HISTORY DOES NOT
REPEAT ITSELF

What we are seeing today is not simply an *economic* upheaval, but something far deeper, something that cannot be understood within the framework of conventional economics. This is why increasingly mystified economists complain that "the old rules don't work any longer." What we are seeing is the general crisis of industrialism— a crisis that transcends the differences between capitalism and Soviet-style communism, a crisis that is simultaneously tearing up our energy base, our value systems, our sense of space and time, our epistemology as well as our economy. What is happening, no more, no less, is the breakdown of industrial civilization on the planet and the first fragmentary appearance of a wholly new and drastically different social order: a super-industrial civilization that will be technological, but no longer industrial.

—Alvin Toffler in
The Eco-Spasm Report

The
ECO-SPASM
Report

by
ALVIN TOFFLER

BANTAM BOOKS
TORONTO · NEW YORK · LONDON

Dedicated to

HEIDI

whose probing intelligence
enriched these pages.

THE ECO-SPASM REPORT

A Bantam Book / March 1975
2nd printing .... March 1975   4th printing .. September 1975
3rd printing .... May 1975   5th printing .... August 1976

Portions of this book first appeared in ESQUIRE
February 1975
All rights reserved.
Copyright © 1975 by Alvin Toffler.
This book may not be reproduced in whole or in part, by
mimeograph or any other means, without permission.
For information address: Bantam Books, Inc.

ISBN 0-553-10181-1

Published simultaneously in the United States and Canada

CONTENTS

AUTHOR'S PREFACE

In 1972, when economic complacency characterized most of the industrial nations, and the world had not yet heard of energy crises, oil embargoes or petrodollars, I began to keep a file on what I casually called the "depression of the future." Into this file I stuck random clippings from the world press, a few economic statistics, as well as a number of interviews with business executives and social welfare officials. I asked them how their organizations might be affected by a depression. By and large, the replies seemed useless: they could not even imagine such an occurrence.

Though engaged in writing a larger work on the politics of the future, I, along with everyone else, soon found the economic situation intruding more and more upon my attention. It was fascinating to see, in little more than a year, how all our longstanding assumptions about affluence, leisure, and unlimited growth could be overthrown. All the rosy expectations of the '50s and '60s, it seemed, were suddenly pushed aside by a growing public dread of what, so recently, had been unimaginable.

In July, 1974 the editors of *Esquire* magazine asked me to undertake a lengthy examination of the next depression. I agreed, but not quite. For I had already decided that my file was out of date; that the depression of the future would not be a depression at all, but something novel, strange, and far more difficult to overcome.

From August through October I traveled—from New Zealand and Australia to Singapore, Beirut and Rome; to Copenhagen and London and back and forth across the United States. I delivered a series of lectures and I interviewed. I talked with a prime minister, many cabinet officials, with economists, businessmen and union leaders, feminists, students and environmentalists, right wingers and middle-of-the-roaders. I attended rallies and read leaflets. And I soon found that my hesitancy about the term "depression" was justified.

And so, I wrote for *Esquire* a lengthy article entitled "Beyond Depression" which looked at today's crisis in the industrial nations and called it, for want of a more descriptive term, an "eco-spasm."

That article, with its dramatic scenarios, forms only a part of this book. Given the stringent space limitations and the conventions of magazine journalism, the article stopped at the bottom, so to speak. It presented essentially a pessimistic view of the crisis and left little room to discuss our positive options and how we might use them.

The article produced a sharp reaction. The term "eco-spasm" instantly began turning up in all sorts of places. Lengthy analyses and critiques of the article appeared in financial journals and newspaper columns. *Esquire* reported receiving more letters and other responses to the article than to any other it had published in years. Yet for many readers, including friends of mine, the article was disappointing in its apparent pessimism. As the futurist John McHale remarked: "too much depression; not enough beyond."

Based on that article but expanded to almost three times its length, this book is a response to my own sense that the criticism was just. New material has been inserted throughout, complex points have been more clearly and fully explained, and a set of "transition strategies" for dealing with the crisis have been added.

Our global problems are decidedly ominous. Our world could end not with a bang or a whimper but with an eco-spasm. Yet we are by no means helpless. I believe these strategies can not only ease the crisis but lead us toward a more just and sensible future.

In summary, then, this book is an interim report, as it were, on the condition of industrial society today, along with some approaches for dealing with it. Researched for many months but written at high speed, with the final pages telephoned from London to New York and published there virtually overnight, *The Eco-Spasm Report* is itself an experiment in what might be called "accelerative publishing." It is being produced, one hopes, in time to help us understand and treat the problem it describes. It is an attempt to deal with serious, complex issues in a compact, readable, reportorial form and in a futurist perspective.

THE GLOBAL CASINO

Money and madness provide two of the great themes of Western literature. Today, as strikes, breakdowns, shortages, and price hikes bombard our consciousness, as bonanza profits and burgeoning unemployment compete for headlines, as stocks gyrate wildly, as inflation and depression contend for dominance, it often seems as though the world money system itself were edging over into madness. Psychiatrists tell us that schizophrenia, one of the most common and dramatic forms of mental illness, is marked by "rapidly fluctuating moods of elation or depression." The victim displays "eccentric concerns about the world and the self." There may be delusions, hallucinations, as well as "insomnia, terrifying dreams, incomprehensible dread." Every one of these phrases aptly describes the economic atmosphere today. For we live in a schizophrenic economy, one that has lost touch with reality. And "incomprehensible dread" is widespread.

In the rolling green hills of Connecticut, in Dorset and Devon, in the fincas outside Bogotá and the farms north of Sydney, apocalyptic nightmares plague the landowners—images of desperate city dwellers cut off from food, medical aid, energy, and water, fanning through the countryside like a pillaging army, squatting on the farmlands, stealing livestock and crops.

In the cities, millions read the headlines with a nervous tic, talk about growing food on rooftops when the supermarkets run dry, and can't help wondering how they will crawl out of the wreckage when the final, cataclysmic collapse occurs.

Until recently, these visions, part Hieronymus Bosch, part Orson Welles, sprang from fear of some ecological upheaval, a collision of industrial societies with the limits of growth. More recently, these fears have fed on economic as distinct from ecological anxiety. Today the talk is of some catastrophic breakdown of the world monetary system. And it is not just long-haired solar-energy or windmill freaks who seek remote hideaways to shelter them for the duration of the anticipated decline and fall. In London, the financier Jim Slater is supposed to have listed what he regards as his basic hyper-inflation survival kit: tinned sardines, a bicycle, a supply of South African gold coins, and a machine gun. A man I know, a leading venture capitalist who has created vast computer companies, and whose business takes him from Park Avenue to Silicon Valley where all the California semiconductors come from, says it will be worse than any of us can imagine. So bad, he says, he is hoarding tennis balls and rackets.

Such sangfroid is not shared by many. James Needham, chairman of the New York Stock Exchange, has warned that "a major capital crisis" could wreck plans for housing, transport, energy development, and business modernization, throw thousands of businesses into bankruptcy, and send unemployment skyrocketing.

Gerald Ford and Henry Kissinger make rumbling threats about the world economy. And Giscard d'Estaing, the French president, says that all the present sociopolitical curves "lead to catastrophe." The *New York Times* sums it up succinctly: "Prophecies that once would have been dismissed as lunatic or vulturish" are now being taken seriously.

Everywhere the question is: Can it happen again? The "it," of course, is the Great Depression that shook the 1930s, beginning with breadlines and ending with

Buchenwald. "1929"—the number is used here as short-hand for the whole decade that followed—crippled a generation and shaped its politics. And we now, in the mid-seventies, await its recurrence. In our astounding innocence, we still believe that history repeats itself. It is as though the world were poised on seat's edge, waiting for an instant replay of yesterday's tragedy. The innocence is poignant. For what lies ahead may be better or worse than "1929." The one thing that is certain is that it will not be the same.

Indeed, what we are seeing today is not simply an *economic* upheaval, but something far deeper, something that cannot be understood within the framework of conventional economics. This is why increasingly mystified economists complain that "the old rules don't work any longer." What we are seeing is the general crisis of industrialism—a crisis that transcends the differences between capitalism and Soviet-style communism, a crisis that is simultaneously tearing up our energy base, our value systems, our family structures, our institutions, our communicative modes, our sense of space and time, our epistemology as well as our economy. What is happening, no more, no less, is the breakdown of industrial civilization on the planet and the first fragmentary appearance of a wholly new and dramatically different social order: a super-industrial civilization that will be technological, but no longer industrial.

Those who insist that what we are passing through is merely a long-needed "correction" ignore all the signals flooding in from non-economic corners of the society. They forget that economic breakdown may be a symptom of a larger transformation and may be generated by forces that economists never think to study. Moreover, precisely because history does not repeat itself, because we *are* moving into a wholly new technoculture, all the carefully constructed "stabilizers" built into advanced economies to prevent a repetition of 1929 are largely irrelevant.

Economists typically cite the existence, for example, of the Federal Deposit Insurance Corporation which insures deposits in 14,470 American banks. They point to the Federal Reserve System in the U.S. or to central banks abroad that presumably prevent bankers from doing anything too foolish. The system of social security payments, unemployment benefits, and pensions, they tell us, will maintain purchasing power in the event of a downswoop. Moreover, in all countries, government employment has now grown so large that it serves as an additional stabilizer, since it is presumably not susceptible to fluctuations of the business cycle. ("If everyone were in the army," one economist explained wryly to me, "there would be no unemployment problem.")

On top of all this, we are told, economists themselves are now far cleverer and more powerful than in those dark, ignorant, computerless days four decades ago. They use complicated computer models of the economy, input-output coefficients, and other miraculous tools for analyzing and forecasting, and they hold influential government positions, having taught presidents, prime ministers, and parliaments how to apply the Keynesian medicines of countercyclical spending, taxation, and credit control. Taken together, it all sounds terribly reassuring—a formidable arsenal of weapons.

Maginot Economics

Yet a closer look reveals that, like generals, economists are busy fighting the last war. Their stabilizers and tools seem increasingly like some cobwebbed, economic version of the Maginot Line—a mighty fortress with guns pointing in irrelevant directions. For all their defenses are premised on the perpetuation of industrial society, not its transformation into something strange, new, and radically different. Nothing in the history of traditional industrial societies has prepared them (or us) for today's high-speed world of instant communication, Eurodollars, petrodollars, multinational corporations, and ganglia-like international banking consortia.

One of the characteristics of this new economic world is the inability of national regulatory mechanisms to deal with transnational economic realities. This came to dramatic attention in April 1970 with the collapse of Bernard Cornfeld's empire, Investors Overseas Services, and a whole series of lesser scandals and hustles based precisely on this weakness of the emerging economic order. By 1968 an estimated 165 "offshore" mutual funds, headquartered in places like Nassau, the Cayman Islands, Liberia, Panama, and the Netherland Antilles, were handling and mishandling billions turned over to them by trusting investors in scores of countries. Operating from mail drops, dummy offices, Hefnerian castles, and even in one case from a yacht called "Give-Up," these ingenious investment managers found themselves delightfully free of governmental regulation. A biographer of the fugitive financier Robert Vesco writes: "This meant that a fund incorporated in Panama but mismanaged from a villa overlooking Lake Lugano in Switzerland by a Greek principal and sold through a Liechtenstein distributor to Brazilian and Scandinavian investors was unlikely to receive much attention in a Panamanian court of law."

The collapse of many of these funds, and the subsequent looting of IOS by Vesco (whose influence penetrated the offices of heads of state in half a dozen countries and who, just to make sure, passed along $200,000 to help reelect Richard Nixon) were, however, only the small, smelly tip of the emerging truth. Colorful as they were, these scandals, defalcations, bum checks, mindless investments, and deceptive annual reports were of limited significance (except to those caught in the wreckage). But they underscored the vast changes that had overtaken the economy since 1929, and they signaled the obsolescence of a part of the Maginot Line.

The very idea of a globe-girdling mutual fund like IOS, which sold shares to thousands of small investors scattered all around the planet, presupposed a previously non-existent middle class in many nations. It also presupposed a level of technological development and communication that would have seemed beyond belief in 1929. Cornfeld's private jet and the computers available to him made it possible to reach far beyond national boundaries and to complete transactions at blinding speeds—to operate, in short, in ways unimaginable forty years earlier.

Almost as radically changed were the new values that arose with the breakdown of the traditional industrial system. Would anyone in the 1920s, at a time when bankers and investment counselors were supposed to be stern, striped, and stodgy conservatives, have dreamed of entrusting a single dollar to an outfit run by a long-haired pseudo socialist who was repeatedly photographed in a headquarters filled with the equivalent of Playboy bunnies? To ask the question is to supply the answer. This was a world for which the regulators and economists, conditioned by the twenties and thirties, were comically unready.

Much more basic were the failure of control measures and stabilizers designed to deal with ultra-legitimate enterprises. For it was not only the bucket-shop dealers and salesmen in blue suede shoes, but bankers of impeccable reputation, who discovered the new freedoms.

They, too, managed to outflank the economic Maginot Line.

Today, although we have central banks, there are so many new banks owned by so many transnational groups or clusters of banks, spread across so many countries, that no one wants responsibility for them. If one consortium bank goes bust, which nation's central bank has to pick up the tab? Does any? How does the U.S., for example, regulate a foreign subsidiary of one of its own banks when that subsidiary may be jointly owned by banks in Japan, England, Sweden, or Germany? And what prevents bankers from legally doing abroad what is regarded as distinctly illegal, if not immoral, at home? (In fact, they do so routinely. At home, U.S. banks are prohibited from "underwriting, selling, or distributing" corporate securities. But overseas many of them do precisely this and operate as if they were Wall Street underwriters, brokers, or dealers.)

How, in this schizophrenic economy, can anyone regulate either the monster banks or the little midges and gnats that operate in their shadows, when each country explicitly refuses to allow anyone else to do the regulating? Martin Mayer, in his recent comprehensive survey *The Bankers,* quotes an official of the Bank of England: "It doesn't matter to *me* whether Citibank is evading American regulations in London. I wouldn't particularly want to know." Mayer tells of two Swedish bank examiners who were literally thrown out of Switzerland—escorted to the airport by police—when they tried to check on the activities of a Swedish bank in Zurich.

And how does top management know what is going on when its bank has grown so large, decentralized, and diversified as to defy detailed understanding? First National City Bank, whose loans and assets have doubled in six years, extracts more than half its profits from some 311 branches or subsidiaries in 65 countries. It has 22,000 overseas employees whose operations are too multifarious and too rapid for effective scrutiny by the home office. And Citibank is by no means alone. Says one Morgan bank official in London: "New York knows what I'm doing because I send them the figures—a week or so late, much too late for them to do anything about it." Under these circumstances, can even the most prudent bank president in Zurich, Osaka, Frankfurt, or New York run a really tight ship?

Bank failures in Germany, Britain, and the U.S. have directed attention to the tightrope the big banks, in particular, find themselves walking—they are over-extended, involved in everything, incapable of digesting their own size, and well beyond the reach of the Maginot gunners. When the Bankhaus Herstatt collapsed in Germany recently, it left behind claims amounting to $100,000,000 or more. When Franklin National toppled —one of the 18 largest banks in the U.S.—it took desperate, barely successful shoring-up measures to prevent total disaster.* *Bank Credit Analyst* not long ago put it bluntly: "In the first seven months of 1974, the [European] banking structure . . . has undergone an upheaval not seen since the banking crisis of the thirties." And as for the U.S., Mayer, after five hundred pages of dispassionate dissection, concludes: "There are billions of dollars of potential loan losses in the system, and the clock ticks toward the moment of their detonation. The

---

* Franklin's controlling interest had been bought in 1972 by Michele Sindona, a shadowy Italian financial operator with close ties to the Vatican, who was subsequently accused of using Franklin to help bail out the near-bankrupt Italian government. After the debacle, the FDIC arranged for the sale of Franklin's cadaver to European-American, a German-Dutch-Austrian-French-Belgian-English consortium. European-American picked up what was worth picking up; the refuse, including some loans that may never be repaid, was dumped at the door of the Federal Reserve Bank, thus passing the problem on to the U.S. public.

banking structure that is now building *can* collapse; the larger the regulatory apparatus permits it to grow, the more catastrophic the collapse will be."

The problem is that this very "apparatus" on which we pin so much faith is now obsolete and no longer capable of controlling the situation. Just how effective are the central banks even within their own countries? When the London & County Securities bank collapsed in England, touching off a crisis among secondary banks, it was quickly discovered that, in the words of the *London Times,* "many of the fringe banks had broken every conventional rule in the banking book," while the Bank of England, drowning in irrelevant data, lacked the new kinds of information systems that might have helped monitor them.

The failure of the old mechanisms and the emergence of new, unregulated forces have turned the foreign exchange market into a garish casino, populated at its edges by gamblers, sheikhs, multinational corporate executives, gangsters, prostitutes, and high-class pimps. Foreign exchange dealers, unmonitored, have speculated on currency fluctuations, losing millions for their banks, while stealing from them on what the *International Currency Review* now terms "a truly massive scale." The *I.C.R.* stoutly reports that they have yielded to "intolerable temptations," including cars and call girls. Central banks have already, in the last five years alone, been hit for an estimated $10 billion, which has been quietly but relentlessly passed on to consumers and taxpayers.

Butterfly Nets

If the world banking system is teetering on the edge of being out of control, one reason lies in the euphonious word "Eurodollars." Like jet planes, computers, nuclear bombs, DDT, and bikinis, Eurodollars did not exist in 1929. They are a product of the transition out of industrialism into a super-industrial (and transnational) civilization. For the uninformed, which includes most of us, Eurodollars are American greenbacks kept abroad in banks but not subject to normal national banking rules. They are a kind of transnational currency.

They are spectral, almost metaphysical. They may consist of "real" dollars—actual currency—deposited in a European or Asian bank. Or they may exist merely in the form of complicated entries on various ledger sheets. An American multinational corporation, for example, may shift $10 million from a bank in Chicago to a bank in Milan. The Milanese bank, with the dollars in hand, may now, on the strength of them, lend out $50 million or even more to a hard-pressed company in Manchester or Marseilles. No actual currency need change hands—no couriers in the night with suitcases stuffed with greenbacks. But $50 million will have slipped into England or France—money over which their central banks have no control.

Thus, very large pools of Eurodollars may build up in Germany or Belgium, or for that matter in the Bahamas, and make all sorts of trouble for the local economy and the politicians and experts who are trying to manage it. Here the "Euros" contribute to inflation, there they shift the balance of payments, in another place they undermine the currency—as they stampede freely from place to place. In trying to damp down their effects, says economist Jane Sneddon Little, author of a short, complicated book on the subject, "central bankers have been in the untenable position of chasing an elephant with butterfly nets." Elsewhere she states: "Not even the wealthiest nations in the world have been able to protect their economies from the meddling of this phantom."

Eurodollars became and remain a problem because so many people have loved them. Russians and Arabs loved them because they provided a way to hold on to dollars outside the U.S.—and therefore dollars that the U.S. government could not, in a fit of political pique, expropriate, as they could if they were actually held in banks in the U.S. Multinational corporations loved them because they were easier to deal with and presumably more reliable than dongs, piasters, dinars, or baht. Bankers especially loved them because they could lend out as many as they liked, as often as they liked, without running up against reserve requirements set by central banks. They could lend them out very profitably, and they could build up larger balloons of credit than they could with real, that is, national (and therefore regulated) money.

Today an estimated 180 billion of such Eurodollars are sloshing around the world money system out of reach of any nation's control mechanisms. The whole swollen Eurocredit system—what one columnist calls "a daisy chain of IOUs"—has mushroomed faster than anyone's ability to understand, contain, or manage it.

Tentacles Everywhere

The growth of transnational banks along with the spectacular rise of the Eurodollar were not, needless to say, accidents of fate. Both arose in large measure to service another new institution: the global corporation, otherwise known as the multinational or (sometimes) the transnational.

Large international companies are, of course, not new. By the early decades of the twentieth century companies like United Fruit, Standard Oil, and International Nickel were doing a global business. Anaconda Copper and Coca-Cola soon entered the lists. From the Netherlands came Philips. From England, Imperial

Chemical Industries and British Petroleum. From Germany, I. G. Farben. From Switzerland, Nestlé. They plucked bananas, dug for oil, packaged chocolate, peddled soft drinks, sewing machines, and the like.

But it wasn't until after World War II, as the age of the telecommunications satellite and the computer network dawned, that American companies invaded Europe on a large scale and touched off the multinational boom. In 1950, U.S. companies had invested almost $12 billion abroad, chiefly in the Western hemisphere and the Middle East, and chiefly in oil and minerals. By 1968 this had shot up to fully $65 billion, of which two-thirds was invested in Europe, and chiefly in manufacturing and trade, not resource extraction. In the sixties, as the tide began to turn against the dollar, a wave of European investment in the U.S. began as well, bringing in firms like Courtaulds, Bayer, and Pechiney.

Today multinational corporations dominate world production. Thus in a 1973 report on the impact of "detente" on the developing nations the Latin American economist Horacio Godoy noted that 140 U.S. multinationals had aggregate sales of $380 billion—a sum larger than the gross national product of any nation other than the U.S. and the USSR. Some individual corporations are economically larger than the countries in which they operate. According to a U.S. Senate Finance Committee study that compared sales to GNP, based on 1970 statistics, General Motors was bigger than South Africa, Ford than Austria, Exxon than Denmark, IT&T than Portugal or Peru. Multinationals operate their own intelligence networks, fleets of planes, and banks of computers. For all practical purposes, they carry out their own foreign policy, often independently of their country of origin. Thus during the 1973 oil crisis officials of Exxon gave Saudi Arabia secret refinery data that was used to cut off the supply of oil to U.S. military units. IT&T prodded the U.S. government to "destabilize" the Allende regime and offered a kitty of funds to the U.S. for that purpose. (The U.S. did not need much prodding, but that is another matter.) More often, multinationals' actions are at odds with the economic policies of the countries in which they operate—and this is not true only of small or feeble developing nations. When the Price Commission in Britain recently refused to grant price increases of up to 50 percent to Shell Chemicals, the corporation threatened to stop selling in Britain.

The multinationals arose to take advantage of what the economists like to call "economies of scale" and "technological rationalization." They could do things more cheaply than smaller companies and they could make effective use of the latest technologies, integrating them across the world. They could stamp out parts in one country, assemble them in another, paint and finish them in a third, warehouse them in a fourth, and sell them in a fifth if they so chose, taking advantage of the special features of each local economy. They could coordinate projects across national lines—often far better than governments could. Early in the game IBM, for example, coordinated work in Germany, Britain, and the U.S. to create its 360 computer. But these were not the only reasons for the rise of the global corporation.

Like the banks that handle their money for them, the multinationals enjoy a freedom of action denied to smaller companies bound by the laws of a single nation. Trying to get a handle on a multinational is like trying to pick up a writhing fish with two fingers. Through "creative accounting" they are often able to shift their tax obligations from one country to another in ways that minimize them. They frequently can escape a nation's labor standards by transferring production to plants located where wages or health and safety requirements are lower.* If one nation sets up stringent anti-pollution controls, the multinational, in principle, can shift production across the border where it can toxify rivers without constraint. Moreover, decisions by the multinationals to accelerate or decelerate payments result in sudden shifts and spurts in the flow of funds across national boundaries, upsetting national plans, payment balances, and currency exchange rates. The men and women who designed our post-Depression stabilizers did so without having the multinationals in mind.

The Temporary Dollar

It was against this background that still another complicating factor arose to change the world economy: "floating" exchange rates—a system of continually changing, transient relationships among currencies, rather than the more stable relationships pegged to the gold standard that previously prevailed. The super-industrial revolution is characterized by accelerated change and by increasing temporariness in personal, informational, and property relationships. The shift to floating exchange rates merely brought the international monetary system into this high-transience world.

After World War II, when Europe was in ruins and the dollar was king, an agreement was hammered out at a conference in Bretton Woods, New Hampshire, that essentially froze the rates at which the dollar could be officially swapped for other currencies. These rates were permitted to fluctuate only the slightest bit—plus or minus 1 percent. The dollar in turn was pegged to a fixed price for gold, and the U.S. agreed to convert dollars

---

* To counter this, many unions are going transnational. The International Federation of Chemical and General Workers' Unions, for example, operates out of Geneva and attempts to coordinate union policies across national lines.

into gold at that price: $35 per ounce. What this boiled down to was a relatively stable system, built around the dollar, in which everyone knew at all times precisely how much a dollar was worth in pounds, marks, or yen.

This relative stability was based, of course, on the pre-eminence of the powerful American economy, in contrast with the weakness of the other capitalist economies. This pre-eminence began to fade as Germany, Japan, France, and other nations revived in the fifties. It diminished even more as U.S. corporations went on a foreign investment binge, pouring dollars into factories abroad and weakening the U.S. balance of payments. The cost of the Vietnam War still further tilted the balance of economic power.

This shift was evident as early as ten years ago to some economists, including Ernest Mandel, a Belgian Marxist, who wrote in 1965 that "total U.S. obligations . . . in other countries are higher today than the total gold stock in the U.S. This means that if all foreign central and private banks were at one and the same time to demand payment, and payment in gold only, not dollars, the U.S. would lose all its gold and the dollar would collapse." He was right.

On August 15, 1971, with inflation battering at the door, with the U.S. balance of payments painfully out of whack, with the real, if not official, value of the dollar dropping, Washington announced that it would no longer promise to deliver gold for $35 per ounce to any central bank or international monetary agency or government that came knocking. Currency exchange rates were fluctuating so wildly all over the place that, four months later, the key governments were forced to let rates "float" up and down. And any pretense of stability was gone.

Since then, monetary conference after conference has passed into oblivion, but the former predictability has never been restored. Rates turn over continually, so that all the relationships between currencies are short-term and quivery. There are complicated, almost theological, arguments about the presumed virtues and vices of floating rates. But, apart from stray insights, no one as yet understands the full consequences of this shift, much less how to deal with it.

Thus, we see how all the old structures and rules of the international economic game—in which every nation's internal economy is now inextricably enmeshed—have rapidly changed. A new global casino has emerged with new and much higher stakes.

Overshadowing all the other players in the world game at this moment are, of course, the oil sheikhs with their "petrodollar" winnings. Never before in the history of the global money system has one group of nations so swiftly, and with such surgical precision, captured so rich a monetary booty, and so destabilized the whole system. Industrial nations are monocultures, wholly dependent upon fossil fuels. The new society must and will have a diversified energy base, just as it will have a diversified social base. In the meantime, however, the need to recycle oil money—to feed it back into circulation without creating catastrophic imbalances of payment—places an even greater unanticipated strain on the banking system and reflects, once more, a situation that could not have occurred in the twenties or thirties. Indeed the problem, says Gary L. Seevers, a member of the Council of Economic Advisers in Washington, "is something economists would not have dreamed of five or ten years ago."

When the Arabs and other oil-producing nations, after years of trying, finally got their cartel effectively organized in 1973 and forced the price of crude oil up by 400 percent in fifteen months, the Middle East seemed about to be overwhelmed by a tidal wave of money. In July 1974 the World Bank estimated that by 1980 the oil-exporting nations would be sitting on top of $653 billion. By 1985, the bank said, this total would rise to $1.2 trillion. In slightly less hysterical times, the U.S. Treasury Department has scaled down these estimates to a mere $200-$250 billion by 1980. This financial accumulation, the new wisdom tells us, is manageable—it can be recycled without utterly destroying the world monetary system.

But while economists argue about such estimates and whether the system is or is not sufficiently flexible to deal with the petrodollar overhang, they ignore a more significant fact that may yet knock all their calculations out of scale. This is the concept of "net energy" introduced by a Florida-based professor of environmental engineering named Howard T. Odum who, in a paper for the Royal Swedish Academy late in 1973, pointed out a simple fact that virtually all the energy pundits and financial wizards had overlooked. In assessing oil reserves and other energy sources available to the industrial economies, all the calculations have been based on *gross* potential, rather than *net*. We estimate that Libya or Louisiana or the North Sea is good for X number of barrels or that the Rocky Mountains could yield X tons of coal. These numbers may or may not be accurate. But it takes energy to get energy, Odum points out, and every offshore oil rig, every mine shaft, or nuclear plant represents an *expenditure* of energy as well as a return.

This means that the quantity of real energy available to us is considerably smaller than usually suggested; and as we are forced to reach for less immediately accessible veins of coal or pools of oil, or more elaborate nuclear installations, the higher the initial energy cost climbs and the lower the net return falls. To ignore this, as has been done until now, is about like doing the bookkeeping for a department store by tallying up the sales and forgetting to tally the wholesale cost of the goods sold.

The picture is by no means clear, but when we begin to look at energy in net, rather than gross, terms, we find that over the past generation or so, since let's say

1929, there has been a sharply rising cost of net energy —net being the only kind we can actually use. Thus M. King Hubbert of the U.S. Geological Survey has shown that if we measure the quantity of oil found for every foot of exploratory drilling, we are getting less for more. In the 1930s in the United States one could anticipate getting 275-300 barrels of crude oil for every foot drilled. By 1970 this had plummeted to 20-30 barrels. One of the striking conclusions of net energy analysis is that in energy terms (not dollars) Arab oil is downright cheap by contrast with the "energy price" we pay for strip-mined coal and nuclear power.

Odum insists that part of the recent inflation in industrial societies can be traced directly to the rising cost of net energy, which he sees as a relentless, fundamental process.

This is not the place for a full-blown discussion of energy and economics and all the alternative sources that could radically alter the picture. It is sufficient for the moment to recognize that a new situation exists—a situation not comparable to 1929, and one for which conventional economics are inadequate.

A Plethora of Shortages

Nothing more starkly underlines the contrast between conditions in the twenties and thirties and those that face us today than a cartoon by Fitzpatrick in the *St. Louis Post-Dispatch* of January 11, 1931. The drawing is divided into three horizontal panels. The topmost panel shows oil rigs belching petroleum into the sky. It is labeled: "Too much oil." The middle panel shows fat, bursting granaries. Its caption complains: "Too much wheat." The bottom panel depicts a soup line and is labeled: "Too much poverty."

Concerned with overproduction, the economists and politicians of the depression era needed to pump purchasing power into the hands of the people in order to increase demand. Today, says economist Leonard Silk, the crisis "stems not from a deficiency of demand but of supply, the most dramatic manifestations of which have been shortages of food and soaring food prices, and shortages of oil and soaring energy prices."

With world population almost twice as large as it was in 1929, and rising rapidly, we are forced to use more and more marginal lands and resources. The global links between population and resources are far more complicated than most studies suggest, and are involved far more with values, politics, class interests, religion, and culture than most analysts admit. The simple Malthusian belief that population *must* outrun resources gives minimal credit to the ability of humans to make a little go a long way by application of cultural or technological imagination. To accept the straight-line projections that lead to doomsday is to capitulate to fashionable gloom. Nevertheless, one does not have to take the apocalyptic plunge to recognize the high likelihood that, along with periodic gluts, we will experience food shortages, and possible shortages of other resources as well such as bauxite, copper, lead, chromite, manganese, and magnesium.

More important, in 1929 the world was still living in the colonial era. Today a wholly new political order is emerging and the days of cheap resources and conveniently docile "natives" are over. The entire power lineup among nations is in for dramatic revision. It may take "wars of redistribution" to bring about this changed structure of global power, but with or without bloodshed the enormous, concentrated power of the great industrial nations, communist and capitalist, is due to diminish, and the power of nations now regarded as poor, "backward," and "powerless" will sharply rise. Nor is this merely the view of left-wing radicals or utopians. It is increasingly recognized in the heart of the corporate world as well. In the words of Dr. Carl Madden, chief economist of the U.S. Chamber of Commerce, we are "going through a great transition, marked by a shift in power between the industrial countries and the raw material-producing countries." Not even the most anti-colonial underground fighter in the 1920s could have hoped for as much.

The Metabolic Burst

Even this catalog of changed economic circumstances does not exhaust the reasons why the future cannot simply replay the past—why the economic crises of the future must be different from those of yesterday. There are two psychosocial factors that must also be taken into account.

First, all the high-technology nations are socially more diversified than they were forty years ago. The number of new occupations has vastly increased. There are also more subcultures, more interest groups, more definable political forces; and regional differences, instead of melting away, are growing more intense. In Britain the Scots and the Welsh are demanding home rule. In Belgium one reads "Pouvoir aux provinces!" scrawled on the highway overpasses. In France the Corsicans and Bretons mutter about secession. In Canada both the Quebecois and the British Columbians, for contrasting reasons, accentuate their differences from the society as a whole. In the U.S. the old melting pot has begun to crack under the blows of a new pluralism. This historic shift toward social diversity is the opposite of the traditional pressure toward uniformity and standardization that characterized the assembly-line era, and it creates a much more complex economy. What this high diversity indicates is that the society is shifting off its industrial base—moving from the monoculture that

was industrialism to the multiculture that will be super-
industrialism. How a multiculture reacts to economic
crisis is very different from the reaction of a monoculture.

A second critical factor that makes the seventies radically different from the thirties is the accelerated tempo
at which problems reach flash point. Every economy
and every political system is geared, whether anyone
notices it or not, to operating at a certain *pace*. Governmental responses to economic change, as well as the
speed of business transactions, are all part of what might
be called a cultural pacing system. Given new communications and transport technology, today's economy probably churns at rates several times faster than was the
case during or preceding the Great Depression.

In *Future Shock* I described the speedup of technological and social change that causes severe personal
and organizational dislocation. This acceleration has
caught up with the economy too. Thus *Fortune* speaks
anxiously about the "stunning speed" with which the
current economic crisis has struck. *Business Week,* citing
figures on credit expansion, writes: "The stunning thing
about the Debt Economy is how rapidly it grew." Even
more "stunning" was the rate of growth of the Eurodollar market described earlier. In the mid-sixties this
pool of money and credit swelled at a rate of 25 percent
per year. In 1969 it reached floodtide proportions, ex-
panding by fully 50 percent. In the next three years the
rate fell off some, but by 1973 it was climbing again by
37 percent per year. Such accelerated growth in almost
anything implies deep adaptational difficulties.

Eurodollars, moreover, not only proliferate rapidly,
or overbreed, they also zip back and forth at electronic
speeds. Economist Jane Little speaks of the formidable
problems their velocity presents to central banks and
refers to "spectacular shifts" as money races from coun-

try to country. These shifts are so swift, she says, that amounts equal to a third of the whole money supply of a country the size of Sweden "can be raised . . . almost overnight." Not surprisingly, *Business Week* finds that "bank disasters," too, unfold at "startling speed."

Corporations now lend out excess funds for periods as short as twenty-four hours, and pension plan portfolios are constantly changing. "Under today's market conditions," says a spokesman for a Pittsburgh manufacturing company, ". . . holding means you're going to get slaughtered."

Not only money but organizational relationships, plans, and people turn over more rapidly as a result of this acceleration. In 1974, for example, the advertising industry in the U.S. saw a 26 percent jump in the number of dollars switched by clients from one agency to another—causing continual upheaval in the ranks. In Detroit, automakers, instead of leisurely planning their advertising campaigns for a year ahead, are forced to work within sixty-day time frames. And in Britain, the Department of Employment issues a puzzled communiqué announcing that between 300,000 and 350,000 people enter and leave the unemployment pool every month—a very high figure in relation to total employment. Across the board, acceleration of change produces a nervous, volatile situation.

Two things, then, happen simultaneously: the system becomes more complex because of diversification and its metabolic rate becomes frenetic. The combination of these two factors—complexity and speed—is explosive.

Systems Overload

Thus we move into the new economic crisis with social systems already overloaded, staggering, and near breakdown from rhythmic and informational as distinct

from purely economic causes. The senile industrial society is dependent upon very rapid, accurately targeted,
intense pulses of information, energy, and money. But
its old structures cannot fire these off in the sequences
required at the necessary speeds. What happens is oscillation.

In classical, 1929-type depressions economies suffered from overproduction; in inflationary times demand
went wild. What is happening today is erratic oscillation between the two, as though a steel cable had been
stretched to its maximum tension and set twanging. One
month the White House or the prime minister talks
about the necessity for a tax increase, the next, about a
tax cut. One day consumers are advised to "whip inflation" by haggling over pennies, buying only what is
necessary, reducing expenditure. The next they are told
it is patriotic to purchase. The Maginot gunners are
swiveling their turrets, uncertain where to shoot next.

In the stock market, these oscillations have led to a
certain grim humor. Years ago J. P. Morgan, asked to
characterize the stock market, dryly replied: "it fluctu-
ates." Today *Financial World* magazine speaks of "fluctuation shock." It reports that "the amplitude of market
movements has accelerated to the point where price
swings normally accomplished in months are contracted
to weeks, weeks to days, and days to hours. How miraculous that the markets discount future events so quickly.
Just think. If the pace continues we will be able to discount the entire twenty-first century by the end of next
week."

Anyone with a sense of perspective ought to fear
extremely rapid price surges as much as sharply plummeting prices; it is the instability of the system that is
revealed. Nor is this wild oscillation confined to the
stock market. Commodity traders, too, are upset. Here
is how *Barrons,* another financial publication, tells it:

". . . many traders betray a nostalgia for the old days of say, three years ago, a yearning for relatively orderly markets and (how to say it?) acceptable price levels. For, strangely enough, they find the extreme volatility upsetting . . . and high prices alarm them too. They remember when a three-cent move in corn was exciting; now, a limit move* is routine, but it's not exciting, it's terrifying."

They have a right to their private terror, for systems analysis tells us that wild oscillation is often a premonitory symptom of breakdown. And these oscillatory movements are evident in other parts of the social system, too. The result: wave after wave of malfunctions and dislocations—postal services, health delivery systems, traffic and transit, police and sanitation services all function spasmodically rather than with the steady, predictable regularity required by the industrial system.

The very complexity of these systems and their interconnectedness increase the possibilities of very large-scale failures. Indeed, systems analyst Roberto Vacca, in what must surely be one of the gloomiest books of the decade, *The Coming Dark Age,* argues that "the proliferation of large systems until they reach critical, unstable, and uneconomic dimensions will be followed by a breakdown at least as rapid as the previous expansion and will be accompanied by many catastrophic events." He imagines a series or convergence of breakdowns compounding one another until a total collapse occurs—as though during the great blackout of 1965, when the lights went out from Canada south to New York, there had also been sudden, unexpected failures of the water supply and the telephone service, and a severe shortage of gasoline, each of these, in turn, lead-

---

* The maximum price change permitted by the exchange in a single day.

ing to further breakdowns and disintegration, until all roads were clogged with unmoving vehicles, water and food cut off, hospitals unable to function for lack of water, oxygen, and electric power, radio and television transmitters silent, and so on. He forecasts the deaths of tens of millions of people—not in Bangladesh or India but precisely in the high-technology nations where dependence on these systems is almost total.

Whether or not one wishes to accept the possibility of such large-scale calamities, the fact remains that the world of 1929 was a much simpler, slower-moving place in which ordinary individuals, even if hungry and job-less, knew more or less where they stood in the scheme of things. Today, under the pressure of rapid change, diversity, and decision stress, this is no longer true. Millions are overwhelmed by uncertainty, their identi-ties fragmented, their loyalties confused and self-can-celing. This psychological fact has decisive *economic* consequences. Thus, says Raymond Fletcher, a member of the British Parliament and vice-president of the Council of Europe, "I do not accept the orthodox view of inflation. . . . I don't think the economic crash creates the social consequences; I believe the social facts could bring about the economic crash.

"Future shock," he says, "has a lot to do with it. People are moving too fast into the future. There's an element of panic in their behavior. They feel they've got to grab everything that's solid here and now, otherwise it's going to run away from them. This syndrome is illus-trated in the dash for sugar—people going to the Con-tinent to buy twelve pounds, twenty-four pounds of sugar, cleaning out the whole of Calais! Everybody wants more, which has always been the driving force behind progress. The difference is they're so frightened of this future that they're being rushed into, that they want it *now* . . . and this phenomenon is much more important as an explanation for inflation than the standard economic argument."

New economic forces, multinational corporations, banks and unions, resource producer cartels, vast pools of unregulated credit, floating rather than fixed currency exchange rates, increased population, powerful new technologies, breakdowns in major service systems, and a subtle but profound change in the psychological conditions of daily life—these, then, form the context in which any economic collapse of the near future would occur. This entire context is radically different from that which framed the disaster of the thirties. The experience summed up in the term "1929" cannot serve as a guide for what lies ahead.

3

OUR OBSOLETE ECONOMICS

Before we can move beyond our 1929 blinders and face the new economic realities, we shall need to break free of the whole set of antique ideas called conventional economics. In a moment we will plunge into a number of dramatic scenarios to see what our immediate economic future may be like. First, however, it is necessary to recognize how anachronistic our thinking is.

This can be seen immediately from the way in which we approach the problem of inflation. Advocates of the left and right argue ad nauseam whether high profits or wage boosts are to blame. Administered prices, high government spending, unjustified expansions of money supply, excess demand, full employment policies—all have been singled out as causes, and a vast technical literature is devoted to their analysis. For the most part, the arguments that rage over these issues could have been conducted quite as readily thirty years ago—and were. Most of the economic research of the past generation has been devoted to sharpening nuances rather than reconceptualizing the entire problem.

Recently, new themes have begun to enter the discussion. The most manifest of these has to do with the cartelization of oil production by the Arabs; among some laymen inflation has come to be regarded as an Islamic invention, rather like the belly dance or the number zero, but infinitely more dangerous. Increasingly the discussion has been forced to take account of the changed population-energy-resources equation, and it is suggested that as more marginal resources and energy sources are called into play, prices must rise.

This fundamental question is just beginning to be taken seriously, but even today most economists seem not to have heard about "net energy" or to have factored it into their calculations.

What all such theories have in common, however, is that they are, in effect, *economic*—and they discuss the economy as though it were hermetically sealed off from the social system, with its swiftly changing values, tastes, sexual behavior, religious views, cultural styles, family arrangements, and organizational forms. Conventional economists look for clues to the inflation problem (and other such problems) solely within the set of measurable abstractions they themselves have created. But reality doesn't come packaged that way. The economy is not a closed system.

Thus I have argued here and elsewhere that one of the really big changes of our time is a profound and rapid shift toward social and cultural diversity in the industrial nations. This splintering of once homogeneous industrial societies both reflects and affects the economic division of labor.

Ever since Adam Smith, economists have sworn that it is highly efficient to specialize, because as Paul Samuelson's classic textbook puts it, it is "better for fat men to do the fishing, lean men the hunting, and smart men to make the medicine. . . ." Industrial societies have carried the division of labor to mind-staggering proportions, and any complaints about its adverse effects are usually focused on the alienation it produces in the worker. Thus Samuelson says, "Specialization may involve some costs, breeding half men—anemic clerks, brutish stokers—and producing social alienation." Such human costs are quickly brushed aside because, it is held, the overall efficiency of the system is radically improved.

Very little attention has been paid, however, to the

idea that there may be upper limits to the advantages of the division of labor, and that we may, at least in certain sectors of the economy, have already reached that stage.

In even the simplest division of labor workers must expend energy on two different functions: one is actually doing the job; the other is maintaining liaison with others who participate in the process. The ditchdigger, the weaver, the spinner, the longshoreman—not to mention the research chemist or stress engineer—must devote some time and energy to this liaison. The digger may say to his buddy, "Hey, a little deeper on the left" or, "Time to get started again!" Even these abbreviated, seemingly simple messages are absolutely essential to coordinating the work of any group.

As the society grows more differentiated, the balance between these two components of work—"production" and "liaison"—shifts, and more energy must go into the liaison component, which is why we have today so many millions of people racing around with pieces of paper—clerks, expediters, supervisors, assistant vice-presidents, coordinators, and bureaucrats. More and more human energy must flow into the process of information exchange in order to maintain equilibrium in the work system as a whole. As a result, there is a fundamental change, not merely in the occupations of people (a decline in blue-collar employment, an increase in white-collar), but a shift in the kinds of personalities preferred in the work force (people who "get along" with others).

This process of white-collarization and the push for what David Riesman termed "other-directedness" are both related, however, to rising levels of social, as distinct from purely economic, diversity. Advancing technology requires more labor division; this, in turn, fosters variety in the population. But simultaneously the new profusion of life-styles, subcultures, ethnic groupings, regional specialties, recreational "affinity groups" all generate demand for a proliferation of varied goods and services.

Contemporary critics of capitalism like Galbraith and Marcuse assert that this is a result of manipulation of the consumer, and that it reflects "false needs." Some of it no doubt does. But the rapid increase in the diversity of material goods and services also reflects the actual shift of the system to much higher levels of social and cultural diversity, the breakup of the homogeneous industrial mass.

This demand for varied new products and services brings with it a proliferation of varied new work processes, alternative work routines for both blue and white collars, so that we wind up with more differentiated, individualized people doing more diverse tasks. And this vastly escalates, once more, the costs of coordination, laying a hidden tax, as it were, on the economy and contributing to whatever inflationary pressures arise from other sources. The problem involves more than money, however; it involves control as well. Thus Hazel Henderson, one of a new breed of "underground economists" who have broken out of the conventional limitations of the field, says: ". . . it becomes increasingly difficult to model the labyrinth of variables in such a web of social and physical systems" and "any system that cannot be modeled cannot be managed."

This is why the arteriosclerotic, moribund industrial societies of both East and West give such an impression of choking complexity and unmanageability. Henderson has invented the provocative concept of "social transaction cost" to suggest that it may be getting harder, in both human and in economic terms, to get *anything* done. It is as though there were an extra barrier of inertia to get through—a rise in internal friction that translates into inflationary cost. Thus, the system, just by trying to hang together a little longer, finds itself faced with a new economic dilemma. To put it another way, she writes: "The proportion of gross national product that must be spent in mediating conflicts, controlling crime, protecting consumers and the environment, providing ever more comprehensive bureaucratic coordination, and generally trying to maintain 'social homeostasis' begins to grow exponentially."

Until economists begin studying the problem of social equilibrium, until they learn how social diversity and new communication patterns and cultural modes impact on the economy, they cannot understand even so relatively simple a process as inflation.

The Economics of Acceleration

Similarly, there are the largely unnoticed effects of the acceleration of change. Today's generalized speedup of the pace of life creates an unprecedented economic situation. Closely related to the new diversity, to population size, higher levels of education, new art forms and communications media, as well as to technological innovation, the accelerative thrust places additional inflationary strain on all industrial economies.

Inflation occurs when the number of dollars in a society increases faster than the products or services available for sale, so that more dollars chase each product or service and drive prices up. (This is why governments try to control the money supply.) But economists have long recognized that the rate at which money changes hands in society is a key variable affecting the level of prices. The faster dollars move from pocket to pocket, the higher the level of expenditures, and for this reason, an increase in the speed with which money circulates— what economists call the "velocity" of money—acts like an increase in the money supply.

The conservative economist Wilhelm Roepke once explained it this way: "A loaf of bread can be eaten only once, but a piece of money can be repeatedly used. . . . The faster the money is passed from hand to hand or, what amounts to the same thing, the briefer are its rest periods in our pockets, the more it can buy within a given period of time." Thus unless the money supply is cut to compensate for it, or the production of goods and services is jumped in proportion, stepping up the velocity of money raises prices. Accelerating the circulation of money is like giving the economy an amphetamine—a dose of "speed."

With the introduction on a wide scale of high-speed computers, improved telecommunication systems, and increased sophistication on the part of multinational banks and corporations, the last decade or two has seen money racing around at very high speeds indeed. But there are other, essentially social, reasons for increased money velocity.

When deep social changes roll through the society at high speeds, they trigger countless adaptations on the part of millions upon millions of people. Individuals buy and sell their homes more often, they hold tag sales and then refurnish, they rent instead of buy, they are moved, promoted, demoted, laid off, rehired, divorced, and remarried—all at accelerated rates. This translates directly into economic amphetamine.

If, for example, we look at the checkbook of a family that is undergoing an important life change, such as a move to a new neighborhood or a divorce or a remarriage or a job change, we are likely to find that many more checks are written just before and after the change than during the period of relative stability in personal life. This accelerated level of personal economic activity reflects the generally accelerated rate of change in society. Multiplied by the millions, it produces faster circulation of the dollar: every dollar changes hands more frequently. And unless this is compensated for by declines in the total money supply or by increases in the total goods and services available, it creates a strong inflationary impact.

In addition, the accelerated way of life has meant the introduction of products with much shorter life spans—more throw-away products, more short-term services, more modular and replaceable parts, more evanescent fashions. This process of ephemeralization of goods and services results in the consumer returning to the marketplace at more frequent intervals than is the case in stable societies, and this too drives up the velocity of money.

If economists, armed with their conventional techniques and conceptual hardware, are having trouble understanding inflation because they ignore its social roots, this is true of other problems: the inability to grapple with so-called "externalities" (the social and economic costs that don't show up on the books), the role of information and organization in the economic process, and scores of other such issues. It is not merely politicians, bankers, and businessmen who are confused; the economists themselves have run into a dead end.

If economics is to help us understand and regulate the new forces buffeting our society, it will have to break out of its narrow, traditional boundaries. It will have to take transnational flows into greater account—not merely flows of money, but of people, ideas, and even psycho-cultural moods. It will have to vastly broaden its concerns with energy and ecological processes. It will have to introduce wholly new accounting systems. It is no longer enough to monitor "national income accounts" or GNP, or to calculate productivity in the old ways, ignoring the economic consequences of social processes like education, housework, or childrearing. Above all, if we are to make sense of where we are and decide intelligently what to do, economics will have to begin paying attention to those two dominant features of the super-industrial revolution—the historic shift toward social differentiation and the continual acceleration of change, often beyond our capacity to cope with it. The result of such expansions and reconceptualizations would be a wholly fresh way of looking at the world— something quite different from what we still call "economics" today.

Factors like these, because they may be hard to measure, because they are complicated, because they are relatively new—and because they lie outside the well-guarded perimeter of conventional economics—are typically ignored or downplayed at present. To repeat, there are distinct social origins of inflation and of many other economic problems. But the economists' microscopes, like their Maginot turrets, are still, by and large, trained in the wrong direction.

4
THE SUPER-INFLATION SCENARIO

Faced with an economic system which no longer resembles the past, which the economists have trouble fathoming, and which is, to a considerable degree, out of control, what are the chances for the near future? What crises might lie in the immediate offing? One way to organize our thinking about such questions is to create a picture of a possible future—to design a "scenario." Scenarios, especially dramatic ones, help organize a vast amount of material into a coherent, plausible form. They show how the present might transform itself into the future.

Given the fact that powerful and conflicting economic and social forces are misfiring today, it is, of course, difficult to predict even short-term swings. Let us look, however, at what might occur if inflation *really* broke loose. Let us look at the super-inflation scenario.

Imagine, for example, not merely an oil embargo, and a doubling and tripling of the price of petroleum and sugar, but spiraling, seemingly endless price hikes affecting a vast array of raw materials—from bauxite to molybdenum, from tin to chromite. Such increases could be brought on by shortages, by uncontrolled, erratic increases in demand, or by the formation of producer cartels. Clearly it will not be easy for the producers to get together, but our world, after all, is full of surprises. Only a few years ago the smart money was betting that the Arabs would never be able to form so powerful an economic bloc. The smart money turned out to be stupid, and that could happen again. If such cartels emerged, the present inflationary shock waves could be exponentially accelerated. Money would pour out of the industrial nations in even greater tidal waves than at present, and prices climb at rates that would make today's double-digit inflation seem fractional.

Imagine multinational corporations and other large companies extremely hard pressed by rising resource prices and forced to borrow vast sums, not for long-term expansion, but simply to stay one jump ahead of the bill collector. Imagine the major powers unable to reach collective agreements on how to respond to the cartelization squeeze, unable to regulate the further mushrooming extension of Eurodollar credits. Imagine trade unions everywhere pressing for increases to keep members abreast of the rising tide of prices, while simultaneously productivity plummets because of shortages, interruptions of electrical service, breakdowns, and delays, some arising from economic causes, others from the increasing unmanageability of large-scale systems. Now, operating under these excruciating pressures, governments surrender their last lingering constraints against printing funny money, and a Niagara of paper money cascades from the presses in Washington. Trillions, quintillions of greenbacks deluge the economy. Tokyo, London, Paris, and Rome follow suit.

More and more, ordinary people mistrust paper. They rush to buy anything—scraps of clothing, diamonds, cases of dog food, used power mowers, snowmobiles, leather goods, baby food—as fast as possible, before prices skyrocket again, thereby creating even more swollen demand and forcing prices even higher. They buy out not only Calais, but Krakow, Kalamazoo, Kyoto. In the controlled economies, black markets flourish despite trials and firing squads. Everywhere else, land turns over at a frenetic rate. Farmers and agro-corporations find their land is worth more than their produce, that they are essentially in the real estate business, not agri-

culture. City services starve. Municipalities find it difficult to sell bonds, even at 20 or 30 percent tax-free.
Schools and police forces are squeezed. Garbage piles
up. Mass transit projects, housing developments, port
and road construction, stadiums and public building
programs are stalled indefinitely because of insanely
spiraling interest rates and the capital crush.

Companies find, to their surprise, that their goods
vanish from the shelves all too swiftly. Sales multiply.
Salesmen, formerly trained to provide a variety of customer services, are reduced to order takers. But prices
rocket up so quickly that many companies find themselves short of funds to purchase raw materials necessary to produce the next round of goods. Trade associa-
tions increase their advertising budgets—but not to encourage consumers to buy; they develop large-scale
strategies and campaigns to damp down demand. They
hire specialists in "de-marketing" and "de-advertising."

The tremendous burst of inflationary forces, all con-
verging at once, further accelerates the rate of change
in society, deepening the uncertainty and sense of tran-
sience. All economic relationships move toward still
shorter and shorter life spans: the durations of loans,
mortgages, union contracts shrink as people, companies,
and organizations fight to avoid long-term commitments. Those with money refuse to put it into thirty-
day paper. Instead, they let it out by the day, by the
hour. Government treasury bills are issued for twelve-
hour periods. Prices are soaring so rapidly that no one
cares what the original marked price of anything was.
What counts is the "multiplier"—the number expressing how many times to multiply the official price.
Thus a bus ticket originally priced at thirty-five cents
may carry a multiplier of a thousand—meaning an
effective price of $350. A gallon of gas costs $700, a
Hershey bar $100. An egg might cost seventy dollars,

or a half hour later a hundred dollars, and if the process continues the digits multiply so precariously that everyone carries a pocket electronic calculator with a minimum display of twelve digits and six or twelve more in its memory. It becomes difficult to visit a massage parlor secretly: the customer wheels a barrow load of cash with him. Kidnappers, meanwhile, up their price like everyone else, and the eight-year-old son of the chairman of the Cost of Living Agency is held for a ransom of $13.6 billion.

It is virtually impossible to write such a scenario without the mind reaching back to Germany, circa 1923, when hyper-inflation broke loose on a hitherto unprecedented scale. Indeed, the picture sketched above is mild and monochromatic in comparison with what actually occurred in the aftermath of World War I. With the victorious Allies, and particularly the French, demanding exorbitant reparations from an already wounded German economy, the value of the mark began to decline vis-à-vis other currencies—and did so at a rate that even today is beyond comprehension. In January 1919, 9 marks could be swapped for one U.S. dollar. In July it took 14 marks, and the following January, 65 marks. But the trouble was only beginning. After some fluctuation the exchange rate reached 190 in January 1922. By then the mark had already lost 95 percent of its value in three years. During the next six months the ratio plummeted again. Now it took 495 marks to buy a dollar, and by January 1923, six months later, it seemed the bottom must surely have been reached. The dollar now fetched an astonishing 18,000 marks—if anyone were willing to take them. From this point on, the retreat of the mark, the plunge toward utter worthlessness, became vertiginous. In July 1923, a single dollar was worth 350,000 marks. By August

the number skyrocketed to 4,620,000. In September it
took nearly 100 million marks to buy what a few years
before could have been had for 9 marks. In October
the mark plunged even further, the bottom dropped
away, and it reached a low point of 25 billion to the
dollar. And by November it reached a number that only
astronomers could contemplate: 4,200,000,000,000
(four point two trillion) to a single dollar.

By now, of course, Germany was gripped by a panic
beyond credibility. Interest rates at the Reichsbank
soared from 5 percent in July 1922 to 30 percent in
August 1923. In September they hit 90 percent. A newspaper that cost 6,000 marks in the morning might cost
130,000 marks when the evening edition appeared.
People fought to get to the head of the line in a store
because the price would be multiplied several hundred
percent by the time those at the end of the line reached
the counter. The printing presses literally could not
keep up with the need for more paper money. In the
final months, more than 30 paper mills operated at full
speed and 150 printing houses with 2,000 presses
worked day and night merely to produce the worthless
bills.

If pressures like these were suddenly to build up
within today's superannuated industrial nations, we
would witness the breakdown of the integrated money
system. In such a situation, let us say, Chicago, Stock-
holm, and Turin begin to issue their own scrip. A Lyons
"livre" can be traded for an Alsatian "fran-marque."
A San Francisco "sutter" (based not on Sutter's gold,
but on municipally held shares of South African gold
mines) replaces the dollar throughout California.
Alaska, with its vast new oil and gas riches, threatens
to secede from the United States in an attempt to cut
loose from the prevailing economic insanity, and barter
becomes a part of everyday life. Ordinary men and

women trade a shirt for a box of cigars, a Chippendale chair for a Burberry raincoat. The *New York Times* prints a series of "Barter Vignettes": one tells of the passenger who gives a London cabby a chicken in payment for a ride to Hampstead. The cabby returns two eggs as "change," whereupon the passenger hands him one egg as a "tip."

Whole subpopulations find themselves wiped out overnight, homes and businesses lost. Pensioners, retired people, civil servants, teachers, and others whose income is fixed or who are poorly organized watch their painstakingly accumulated savings, their economic life's blood, drain away as though from an ax gash, their dollars, rubles, marks, yen, or kroner rendered meaningless, their former social status destroyed in a stroke.

The impact of inflation reaches deep into the individual psyche too. Inflation, according to psychiatrist William Flynn of Georgetown University, leads to "exaggeration of personality patterns that have pre-existed." Some people adopt a devil-may-care, live-to-the-hilt attitude, others become calculating and conservative, others suffer severe depression, and still others search for scapegoats upon whom to unleash aggression. Inflation, under this theory, acts as a kind of psychological monosodium glutamate, accentuating whatever flavor happens to be there, for good or for ill. But virtually all psychologists and psychiatrists agree that inflation sharply increases the stress load. Says Dr. Alathena Smith, a Beverly Hills psychologist, "If they're unstable, it's going to unstabilize them sooner. An elastic band can only be pulled so far." Cost-related pathologies skyrocket in price. The annual cost, for example, of a heroin habit has already zoomed from $22,000 to $29,-000 in one year in the U.S.

One might, of course, extend this scenario at will, sketching in more and more detail, drawing on Germany as a model. But if the future will not replay the Great Depression, it is also unlikely, for multiple reasons, to replicate the German experience. Unlike the Allies, who demanded and got their reparations from Germany in the form of hard goods—gold, railroad cars, locomotives, boats, submarine cables, machinery, horses, bulls, sheep, trucks, and the like—the Arabs, so far, have received only paper for their petroleum. They now must help prevent the collapse of the industrial economies if that paper is to be worth anything. Moreover, the German hyperinflation did not just happen by accident. It was deliberately engineered by a government more interested in crushing the domestic left wing than in preserving economic stability, and the industrialist Hugo Stinnes, one of Germany's capitalist overlords at the time, spoke of using "the weapon of inflation" to save Germany from bolshevism.

Most important, however, the German hyper-inflation was just that: a runaway inflation essentially contained within the boundaries of one nation. Today the entire industrial world is caught in a violent inflationary spiral that spares no one. The economic system has become overly interdependent, so that there are no innocent bystanders. This means, as well, that in the event of collapse there will be fewer external sources of new capital to pull us out.

The money system could collapse; money could, indeed, become worthless as some of the more apocalyptic prophets warn. Economically speaking, very little is *impossible* these days. But if it happens, it will be infinitely different from the German experience of 1923. Too many fundamental factors have changed irreversibly. In short, the symbol "1923" is as inappropriate as the symbol "1929."

5

THE GENERALIZED DEPRESSION SCENARIO

A Manhattan real estate attorney, asked recently by me how his business was, replied with a thin smile: "A catastrophe moving toward a holocaust." And, of course, the signs of depression are easy to find in many countries. Rapid increases in unemployment in the U.S. and Australia, rising bankruptcies in Japan, foreign workers being sent home by Germany, travel company failures in England, plants closing in Singapore—all suggest a sharp downward break in the industrial economies. What might happen if the bottom does, in fact, fall out? Once again, a scenario can help us picture the consequences.

To say that 1929 will not recur, as I have argued above, does not mean that a depression is impossible. It simply means that not all depressions are alike. Indeed, 1929 has so badly colored our thinking on the issue that we normally ignore the many other possible forms that such an event might take—at least as many as the Asian flu. Out in the desert, at Phoenix College in Arizona, an imaginative futurist named Billy Rojas and a group of his students have put together a simple typology of depressions that includes the following types:

1. *Depression on the Installment Plan*—in which various sectors of the economy collapse seriatim rather than simultaneously, each of them declining and coming back to life at different intervals.

2. *The Sleeper Depression*—in which a gradual, worsening decline affects the entire economy over an extended period, a so-called crashless depression.

3. *The Magic-Formula Depression*—a 1929-type debacle which, however, ends almost as soon as it starts because the government solves the problem by applying precisely the right remedies at precisely the right moments. (Otherwise known as the don't-count-on-it depression.)

4. *Super-Crash*—in which everything collapses at once, and unemployment bounces as high as 25 to 50 percent.

5. *Armageddon Depression*—a short depression followed by global war. (Self-explanatory.)

To deny that one or another of these calamities is possible requires an intensity of faith commonly associated only with saints and teenage followers of Guru Maharaj Ji. It is not difficult, therefore, to imagine the following events within the next half-decade or less. (Given the multiple forms a depression can take, one ought, properly speaking, to trace an alternative scenario for each. To keep it simple and relatively short, however, we confine ourselves to one.) Here then is what might be called the "generalized depression scenario."

Imagine, if you will, that a nervous, harried Republican administration in Washington, confronted by rioting farmers and raging consumers, takes "strong countermeasures" to control inflation, "the nation's number one enemy." (With modifications, the same scenario could be adapted to France, Germany, England, Australia, Japan, or any number of other countries.) Continuing to think in conventional categories, the government tries to slash consumer spending by forcing through a tax increase. Unemployment, if not exactly welcomed, is permitted to climb and does so—but faster than anticipated. Auto and major appliance sales skid further downward and layoffs worsen in these industries. Democrats, as part of the deal for a tax increase, compel cuts in defense spending, resulting in a wave of white-collar and engineer layoffs in southern California, Seattle, and Long Island. Tightly organized construction workers extract a 42 percent across-the-board wage hike to "keep up with inflation" but rentals and home sales are down sharply. Several giant office building and home development companies, caught in the squeeze, fall into receivership, leaving three big banks holding worthless IOUs to the tune of some $150 million. As the late-night editions announce this in forty-eight-point type, thousands begin queuing up outside the branches of the affected banks.

Now the government, through the FDIC, steps in to halt what looks menacingly like the start of a run on deposits. But television camera crews have already pictured mobs gathering outside the stricken banks, and lines begin to form at hundreds of other banks overnight. Anticipating a hailstorm of claims, FDIC officials know what most of the public doesn't: that the agency has only enough money on hand to cover about 1 percent of deposits. It cannot possibly meet a wild, runaway demand by hundreds of thousands of terrified bank customers. Top policy makers hold a hurried early morning meeting to consider an announcement that the FDIC will pay all claims entered before the close of the previous banking day, but from now on will insure accounts only up to $10,000, instead of the $40,000 hitherto guaranteed. This policy is flatly rejected after hasty consultation with the White House. Intense conferences and telephone calls turn the agency headquarters and the Federal Reserve Bank into twin madhouses.

At twelve noon the major television networks receive calls from the president's office asking them to clear immediate air time for an emergency message. By 1:10 p.m., the president is in front of the cameras. In the streets of Manhattan, in Battersea pubs, in apartments in Neuilly, and elsewhere in the appropriate time zones millions crowd to their television screens for the live satellite transmission. The president seems calm, self-assured. His tone is grave but firm. After describing the latest economic news, he comes to the crux of the matter: "No citizen will lose a single penny as a result of this latest unfortunate development. The banks of this country are sound.

"The government stands ready to back that claim with all its resources. The nation is rich, its technological and human power as solid as ever before. It needs only to be marshaled.

"To deal with the immediate problem, the Federal Reserve Bank stands ready to assume all outstanding debts of the threatened banks.

"However, due to the unusual circumstances, all banks in the nation will close down for one week to give their overworked employees and federal officials time to catch up with the unusual load of paperwork.

"During this week, a moratorium will apply to all debts so that no debtor, not even the poorest, will lose as a result. There is nothing to fear except . . ."

By 3:00 p.m. it is evident that the president's remarks have been partly successful in allaying the panic. The lines outside the banks begin to dwindle, although some stubborn folk linger hopefully on. But Wall Street's instantaneous reaction is different. Even as the president's first words began fleeting across the ticker tape, the selling began. Within minutes it had become a surging, thunderous stampede, overloading the tickers, the people, the mind itself. By the next afternoon, as the results begin to sort themselves out, the news is stark: the market, which had been zigzagging downward for weeks, has crashed well below the Dow-Jones 250 line.

As the week wears on, drained faces and numbed nervous systems follow the accelerating crisis. Pension funds, one of the most vaunted stabilizers, see their port-folios shrivel in the all-consuming fire, and suddenly find themselves unable to meet commitments. The Labor-Management Fund for the steel industry, one of the hardest hit, announces it will be forced to cut pension payments by 15 percent for the next three months at least, and other funds, once the ice is cracked, follow suit. Some announce insolvency. Workers who have spent forty-five years in a steel mill or a telephone exchange, or who have bucked heavy loads on the docks, now take to the streets. Newspapers report what they call the "Pension Riots," and "gray revolutionaries" demand a government takeover of all pension obligations.

Meanwhile, the social security system, with $2.1 trillion worth of unfunded obligations, sees its income slashed as layoffs mushroom. The administration, aware that the slightest reduction of social security payments would turn the pension riots into a massive, irretrievable disaster for the country, hastily announces plans to float bonds to shore up the system, with the Federal Reserve undertaking to purchase them. Economists recognize this as a further desperate resort to the printing press. Simultaneously, as joblessness reaches new highs, unemployment benefits are exhausted and purchasing power falls far below the level originally forecast by the government's economists and planners. Hundreds of thousands, even millions of families find themselves suddenly and swiftly forced down to pre-affluence levels of living, and the vast bubble-gum balloon of consumer credit—the magical money that underwrote auto purchases, trips to Hawaii, St. Tropez, or Malta, second homes, color television sets and electric hair dryers—suddenly begins to collapse. And now, at last, comes the long-awaited deflation. Like pressure suddenly escaping from an airliner's smashed window, sucking meal trays, seats, suitcases, and passengers out with it, the inflationary pressures whoosh out of the closely integrated industrial economies. The end of the paper economy has been reached. The generalized depression begins . . .

In New Orleans the local transit company, which in response to federal lawsuits has started hiring women bus drivers on an equal basis with men, announces it will lay off 50 drivers. Following standard union seniority arrangements, the last hired are the first to go. This means that of the 50 victims, 38 are women—and they refuse to go. At 4:00 a.m., before the start of the morning shift, 30 women with 6 male sympathizers begin picketing the main bus depot. Their signs demand a "fair chance to work." It is a cool, turquoise morning, and when the first few male drivers arrive they exchange banter with the women. By 5:30, with 100 men milling about outside, laughing, shouting wisecracks, and shifting restlessly from foot to foot as starting time approaches, the women are still resolutely blocking the gate with their bodies. They plead, argue, cajole, and insist that they need the jobs as badly as the men do. More than half of them are divorced, widowed, or single, most with children at home dependent upon the mother's paycheck.

As the clock ticks on, the banter turns sour. Shouts of "Get a husband!" and "Go home to your kids!" resound. No one knows who strikes the first blow, but in minutes the street in front of the main gate is turned into a raging maelstrom, with the women drivers furiously punching, scratching, and screaming their desperation. The men, despite initial embarrassment, soon curse and strike back. Arms and legs fly, hair is pulled, faces bleed.

By now, photographers from the *Times-Picayune* and the *States-Item* are snapping away, enjoying the scene. TV news trucks roll up, along with police cars and ambulances. The women, quickly overwhelmed by superior numbers, promise to come back the next day with thousands of their "sisters" to support them. The men jeer and force their way into the carbarn and the buses begin to roll out. Meanwhile a few women are interviewed. Some are tear-streaked, others stonily defiant.

The following day 1,000 women turn up at the gate. It is the first of the direct sexual confrontations that, in the weeks ahead, spread like grassfire across the country. Headline writers lament the loss of "chivalry." Feminists burn their union cards in protest against the traditional seniority rules. Women police refuse to serve on picket line duty. The First Women's Bank of Denver sets aside a special fund for low-interest emergency loans to striking women.

At the Diplomat Hotel in Manhattan, meanwhile, and simultaneously at the Jack Tar in San Francisco, two conferences are held and connected by telephone lines. At these meetings leading professors from Berkeley and the New School for Social Research, along with students and a number of local labor leaders, join Michael Harrington in issuing a call for a new American Socialist Party. In Los Angeles, at almost the same time, a well-known investment counselor hurls himself out of a twelfth-floor office window, having first thrown a fire extinguisher through to smash the glass. He lands on Wilshire Boulevard and suddenly all the old depression jokes are revived, including the Eddie Cantor classic: Broker enters hotel and asks for room. Room clerk asks in return: "For sleeping, sir, or for jumping?"

At this point, the standard 1929 scenario can be plugged neatly in, for it illustrates in great detail what happens when jobs vanish and prices fall, when loans are called, mortgages are foreclosed, repossessions mount, and money—real money—comes back into fashion because of its scarcity. It tells us in graphic detail what happens to children without food, to Ph.D.'s forced to rake leaves, to millions of restless men shifting back and forth across the landscape in search of the elusive job. It tells us that fortunes are undone overnight, that misery and fury stalk the country.

6

ECO-SPASM

What the standard descriptions of depression tell us, however, may well be misleading. For just as the 1923-type inflation no longer provides a useful guide to the present, so, too, the idea of a single, sweeping, generalized depression may turn out to be far too simple.

To draw on the experience of 1929 involves a fundamental error—the confusion of depression with deflation. It is, of course, still possible that the present queasy situation will collapse into a general deflation. But what we are more likely to see in the immediate future (what, indeed, we are already beginning to see) is not the classic breakdown and deflation, with both employment and prices collapsing in tandem. What we may have to confront is something that will be radically different—and potentially much worse. Not an inflation, a depression, a boom, a bust, or a recession, or even "stagflation," but what might be called an "eco-spasm."

The eco-spasm or spasmodic economy describes an economy careening on the brink of disaster, awaiting only the random convergence of certain critical events that have not occurred simultaneously—so far. It is an economy in which powerful upward and downward forces clash like warring armies, in which crises in national economies send out global shock waves, in which former colonial powers and colonies begin to reverse roles, in which systemic breakdowns aggravate economic disorder and economic disorder intensifies and accelerates systemic breakdowns, in which "random" ecological and military eruptions hammer at the economy from different directions, in which change piles upon change at faster and faster rates, creating tensions never before experienced in high-technology societies.

Harold Strudler of the Institute for the Future, who uses the term "eco-spasm" in this sense, calls it also the "hysteresis economy"—an economy in which all the systems lag at different rates, creating increasing disorder and uncertainty. To grasp the meaning (or meaninglessness) of such an economy, imagine for a moment the possibility of 1923 and 1929 occurring simultaneously, as though through some aberration in the time stream. Imagine not merely the soft collision suggested by such euphemisms as stagflation, but a combination of erratic super-inflationary forces and super-depressive forces striking at once. This combination produces two additional categories of depression in the Rojas scheme of categorization: depressions number six and seven.

6. *Selective Depression*—in which sectors A, B, and C collapse for the duration, but sectors D, E, and F stay healthy or even grow.

7. *The Mobile Depression*—in which the depression migrates from region to region, city to city, quickly, while inflationary booms move in just behind or ahead of it.

But if we wish to understand a full-fledged eco-spasm, we must see this alien economic landscape in a context of highly erratic ecological, military, social, and cultural events. It becomes possible to create a matrix out of these possibilities, say, a blinking display in which red lights flash for a depression, green lights for inflation, and multicolored additional lights for other forces, with the lights flashing and flickering so rapidly and seemingly at random that no government policy is capable of keeping up. Indeed, precisely such a world is now already swiftly emerging, not just in the U.S. but in most industrial nations. Workers at Fiat and Philips, at GM and Nippon Kokan are working short hours or being sent home by the thousands. In several nations joblessness is pushing the one million mark conventionally regarded by them as the social danger point. In the U.S., the level thrusts above 8 percent—the highest since 1941. The extreme volatility of the situation is underscored by the fact that when this passage was first drafted the rate had barely passed 6 percent. By the time it reached print in magazine form a few weeks later it was already out of date. At this writing no one can be sure that the rate won't crack the 10 percent line. Total elapsed time: ninety days.

All this should mean lowered wages and reduced job opportunities across the board. Yet in England, for example, the unemployment in many industries contrasts starkly with a kind of hyper-prosperity in others. Raymond Fletcher, the British M.P. who represents Ilkeston, the district immortalized by D. H. Lawrence in *Lady Chatterley's Lover,* predicts a "really impressive advance . . . in some industries side by side with stagnation and crack-up in others." In his own constituency, he says, "there's a terrible labor shortage and skilled engineers can literally demand any price they want for labor up in Birmingham. I visited a plant where they make plastic fitments—everything from great big garage doors to little hors d'oeuvre forks—and they cannot get enough people to fill all the orders they're getting from abroad. But elsewhere, the jobs disappear. . . ." Nor does high unemployment force prices down as it should if a classical deflation were occurring. One can scarcely shoulder one's way through the throngs on Oxford Street in London where Marks & Spencer, Selfridges, and other department stores line the way. Chichi clubs like Annabel's and the White Elephant do a roaring, last-days-of-Pompeii business.

In Italy the government is virtually bankrupt. It has cadged nearly $17 billion from abroad to stay afloat, money which, according to former treasury minister Emilio Colombo, has vanished like a "drop of water on a hot stove." Yet the Via Veneto is jammed with tourists and shoppers, the hotels are over-booked, money is everywhere in evidence among the upper classes, and one economist—a top official of one of the nationalized industries—seriously predicts that Italy will become a great and rich world power in two or three years because she sits astride the Mediterranean between Arab oil and an energy-starved Europe. In the U.S., construction workers are laid off; oil workers experience boom times; Detroit in the doldrums, Wyoming preparing for a resource boom. The whole thing, says Henry Boettinger, chief of planning for the Bell Telephone System, "is like a great roulette wheel."

This massive roulette is already producing fantastically varied effects, intensifying diversity not merely among nations but among regions and even individuals. At the very moment when Buffalo, New York, suffers from an officially acknowledged unemployment rate of 10.3 percent (and a real rate closer to 20 percent), Cedar Rapids, Iowa, reports only 3 percent out of work with retail sales rising. While Lewis Hawkins, an unemployed twenty-eight-year-old concrete finisher, says bitterly, "There's going to be a lot of stealing, a lot of mugging and everything" as people like him go hungry, and Rosie Washington, a jobless administrative assistant with a six-year-old daughter to feed, predicts, "We're going to have a revolution . . ." hotels and motels with some 27,000 rooms around Disneyworld in Florida enjoy a walloping 93 percent occupancy rate, and the U.S. Department of Commerce receives a detailed study forecasting the rise of "boom towns" in the Mountain states.

Houseware manufacturers report big gains in sales of

"quick-drip coffee makers" and "pistol-grip hair dryers" while Manhattan office buildings sit with 28.6 million square feet of idle office space. Richard R. Violette of the U.S. Defense Security Assistance Agency, the chief arms merchant of the U.S. government, is doing a rip-roaring business selling tank parts to Turkey, ballistic missiles to Israel, and other weapons to Oman, Iran, and Saudi Arabia, while police in Los Angeles train special "crowd control squads" in anticipation of violent protests arising out of the economic situation and Caribbean resorts burst with American tourists. The net effect is of some schizophrenic dreamworld.

Picture now, if one can, an American president facing re-election as the eco-spasm approaches and unemployment in the industrial belt around the Great Lakes continues to rise—in Buffalo, in Erie, in Cleveland, Toledo, Detroit, South Bend, and Chicago. The level reaches 12, 15, even 20 percent among white males. Among black workers under age twenty-one, the level hits 50 percent. Union agreements guarantee laid-off auto workers "supplemental unemployment benefits" to be paid by the employers, but the Big Four auto companies, with sales plummeting to new lows, call a special meeting with the United Auto Workers to discuss cutting back on these payments. Immediately, the UAW demands that the federal government insure workers against defaulted SUB payments.

The president agrees to approve such a measure, and the House, moving with alacrity, passes a bill in response. But the Senate dawdles. The president, in the meantime, promises increased aid to the stricken cities, increased hiring by the government as "employer of last resort," special programs to keep "minority youth" off the streets, and all the while prices continue to rise. He suggests that new taxes will be needed to help pay for

these programs if the federal deficit is not to exceed $85
billion, but with food costs, auto prices, travel expenses,
medical services, the price of housing all zooming, any
serious attempt to enact a tax measure must be post-
poned till after the election.

Suddenly a wave of personal bankruptcies sweeps
through the nation, soaring to the rate of 60,000 per
month, as dentists and dockworkers, young married
couples and retirees find it impossible to pay their bills.
A senator from California proposes creation of a Federal Loan Insurance Corporation to guarantee credit
card companies and other lenders against bad debts
so they can continue to extend credit to "keep the wheels
of America moving." The Burpee Seed Company, sales
and profits both rising steeply as fears of a food shortage
deepen, announces acquisition of the Ball Corporation's
glass jar division and their consolidation into a new
company to be called Survival, Inc.

In the meantime, coal mines in Utah, ready for increased production, find it impossible to recruit trained
miners, and in the East a sixteen-day coal strike para-
lyzes industry from Maine to Maryland. The president
agrees to meet with the six New England governors who
want a crash program to ship coal east from reserves in
the South and Midwest. But Governor Harris of Colorado, himself facing re-election, refuses "to let one ton
of coal leave my state until the federal government can
assure us that *our* people will not go cold this winter."
Canada agrees to release additional supplies of fuel oil
from its own reserves, but nationalists there insist that
the price be pegged to the "OPEC price plus one penny"
—plus processing costs and profits. In New York, the
smash production of *The Pioneer Woman,* starring
Robert Redford and Liv Ullmann, has created six-deep
lines around so many movie houses that *Variety* reports:
PIONEER OUTSHOOTS GODFATHER. Tickets are

going for $6.50 each and are being scalped for $25. Downtown, the stock market, despite outrageous super-profits in certain industries, continues its precipitous descent.

Only buying by Arabs, Indonesians, Iranians, Venezuelans, and (through intermediaries) Russians has kept the Dow-Jones above the 300 line until now. As it plummets below the 350 mark, bargain hunters from the oil-rich nations, along with some Soviet specialists, begin picking off the plums. Venezuela grabs a controlling share of the *Miami News*. Iran wryly captures *Harper's* magazine in retaliation for an article by Frances FitzGerald. Arabs purchase controlling positions in some insurance companies, buy a substantial block of Time, Inc., and foray less obtrusively into plastics manufacture (including some sub-contractors producing jet aviation parts), and real estate. The Russians, through thinly veiled Swiss fronts, buy into ConAgra and other major agro-corporations whose lobbies influence government policy on food exports. The Indonesians, for their part, pick up shares of Northwest Orient Airlines at far below book, and own hotels in Manhattan, Washington, and Beverly Hills. It is there on October 10 that a bomb rips through the lobby of the Jakarta Imperial, wounding three Japanese tourists and the night manager. Station KNXT-TV receives a tape on which a woman with a heavily accented voice claims credit for the bombing, identifies herself as a captain in the Indonesian Liberation Army, and signs off, "Down with Suharto!"

In mid-October, with rents rising across the country, 150,000 marchers descend on Lafayette Park to demand nationwide rent controls. A discreet message to the White House from the powerful Arab real estate lobby, through its Washington lawyers, Reilly, MacIntire, and Greenberg, suggests that any attempt to control rents would meet with instant retaliation in the form of reduced oil allotments.

A few days later, the Food and Drug administrator, Harold Whitwell, requests a meeting with the president on a matter of the "utmost pressing urgency." Whitwell begins by handing the president a 382-page blue-bound report stamped "Top Secret" which proves beyond dispute that a disaster is in the making. Tens of millions of jars and cans of baby food now circulating in the market have been found to contain Arceon Yellow, a dye which tests now show to be the cause of serious mental retardation in infants. The president, after consultation with his election strategists and television specialists, moves swiftly.

That evening, in a special television appearance, he explains that while there is no cause for alarm he is, as a precautionary measure, asking all baby-food manufacturers using Arceon Yellow to suspend production, and all supermarkets and local stores to remove from their shelves all bottled or canned baby-food products until tests can conclusively show them to be pure. He is also asking all producers of commercial Zeronacephon, a safe but expensive substitute for Arceon Yellow, to halt immediately all shipments except those to baby-food manufacturers, to guarantee that consumer supplies can be resumed as safely and speedily as possible.

Plastics manufacturers, who require Zeronacephon for many of their products, immediately protest and begin besieging Zeronacephon producers for stepped-up shipments and emergency supplies. The price of bulk Zeronacephon zooms from $12.20 per barrel to $33.82, and the shares of Texsyn Corporation, the prime manufacturer of Zeronacephon, leap from 4¾ to 12. Meanwhile, pediatricians' offices are jammed by mothers who think their children may have already been affected.

Texsyn Corporation is not the only one doing well.

Makers of automatic generators, halazone tablets, solar heating units, camping equipment, and rifles all report operations at full capacity and profit increases ranging from 41 to 380 percent over the preceding year. Despite this, the mood is somber, and on October 20, the Council of Economic Advisers, the Treasury Department, the Federal Reserve, and the reconstituted Cost of Living Agency jointly announce that for the duration of the crisis all federal officials above the rank of GS-18—that is, all political appointees as distinct from civil servants —will work a ten-hour day without additional pay. The secretary of the treasury is photographed saying goodbye to his chauffeur and his Lincoln Continental Limousine and stepping into a Chevrolet Vega which he proposes to drive himself. (He receives a telegram of protest that afternoon from the Lincoln Division of the Ford Motor Company, charging favoritism to GM, along with one from the Teamsters Union.) Meanwhile, the newly formed National Unity Committee (cochaired by David Rockefeller of Chase Manhattan and George Meany of the AFL-CIO) urges all Americans to "pull together" in this mounting national crisis.

Marijuana Cool

Nevertheless, on Thursday, October 27, fighting occurs outside the gates of the Cuyahoga Bicycle Company in Cleveland, Ohio, where the employment office is hiring 700 additional workers to step up production. Demand for bicycles is outrunning the industry's capacity to produce. But 4,000 unemployed workers have turned up for the jobs. Scuffling has turned into an ugly riot between blacks and whites and spilled into the streets. By nightfall, a six-block area is in flames and state troopers and National Guard units have moved in. They can no longer contain the rioting.

The following afternoon, at 3:35 p.m. EST, as the president ponders a request from Governor Scott for troops to be sent to Cleveland, the first news arrives of an attempted coup in Saudi Arabia. Catching both the CIA and the KGB off guard, a group of left-wing colonels announce that they have taken control of the radio stations and key military positions, and that the palace of King Faisal is under assault. The attack is lightning swift, and by midnight, when the king's capture seems imminent, U.S. cruisers in the eastern Mediterranean intercept a warning sent by Faisal to the rebels. Failure to withdraw will lead to the destruction of the petroleum wellheads—a potential catastrophe beyond quantification. Within the hour, the demand is rejected, and a squadron of loyalist jet bombers streaks into the sky. As a symbol of Faisal's determination, they drop their bombs on the Aramco Marine Terminal at Ras Tanura, where dozens of huge storage tanks, one after another, explode into the night. An enormous shuddering earthquake is felt at a distance of more than fifty miles. Unless the rebels lay down their arms, Faisal announces, the wellheads themselves will go next, leaving nothing for the colonels to govern but scorched sand dunes. Satellite observation photos, placed on the president's desk within hours, reveal massive destruction, flames still roaring into a blackened sky. American naval forces begin to converge on the scene from the Mediterranean and the Indian Ocean, and the secretary of state, warning unspecified other nations "not to take advantage of this unfortunate crisis in the Middle East," announces that all U.S. forces have been placed, once more, on nuclear alert.

Back home, the Senate again defers action to aid the jobless auto workers, but Pentagon requests for a new super-MIRV program and several additional new weapons systems rocket through almost without debate. At Rockwell International Corporation in Columbus, Ohio, at McDonnell-Douglas in Huntington Beach, California, at RCA and GE plants in New Jersey and Pennsylvania, recruiters cannot find enough engineers and trained technicians. Simultaneously, however, San Francisco announces that, for the first time, its unemployment rate has hit 15 percent. Municipal soup lines are set up to serve stew along with (legalized) marijuana. The *San Francisco Chronicle* congratulates the city on its foresightedness and the "social use" of marijuana to cool tempers during difficult times. The *Examiner,* however, lashes out in an editorial entitled: "Stop the Hash and Hash Handout!"

In Washington, Republicans charge that the Democrats are "as usual, the war party and the party of inflation." The Democratic party countercharges that Republicans want to see Hoovervilles re-established around the United States. Consumers occupy supermarkets in Austin and Atlanta, burning baby food and demanding price reductions. Fighting has now also broken out between farmers in Iowa and representatives of the big packing companies. The farmers are refusing to accept paper dollars for their hogs. They threaten to kill 10,000 pigs in protest and dump their carcasses into the Mississippi unless the giant packers and supermarkets fix a new price and pay them in so-called C-Opecs —crude-oil equivalents, units of scrip worth fixed amounts of crude.

In Manhattan, the Excelsior Cooperative on Fifty-seventh Street announces that its board of directors has authorized the purchase of a farm in upstate New York that will provide "guaranteed food supplies, including dairy products" for the residents of the high-rise luxury building. Each tenant has been assessed $2,000 for that purpose. In the future, when a tenant sells an apartment, shares will include part ownership of the farm.

An advertising executive in San Francisco runs an ad recruiting "survivalists" to join his "long-range shelter commune" in the wilds of northern California. Applicants must come equipped with a "three-year supply of everything." His postman complains that he cannot carry the load of incoming mail by himself. And in Newark, New Jersey, preparing for the food shortage, residents tear up several paved streets, cordon them off with barbed wire, and begin planting tomatoes, carrots, and zucchini.

On the night of October 30, seismologists and nuclear radiation experts at the Lawrence Livermore Laboratory in California and at CERN in Geneva report evidences of a nuclear explosion of "great magnitude" on the shores of Lake Baikal in central Russia, in the vicinity of one of the Soviet Union's experimental fast-breeder reactors. News of the explosion reaches the White House almost immediately, although physicists at the Atomic Energy Agency say they can give few details. It is an apparent accident. If their calculations are correct, civilian casualties could be enormous. No reliable measures of escaped radioactivity are available as yet. But in all likelihood winds are carrying the contaminated air toward the Chinese border. At 1:00 a.m., a hot-line call to Moscow confirms the accidental nature of the eruption. The U.S. offers emergency aid; the Russians spurn the offer.

The following morning, as he leaves his driveway in Falls Church, Virginia, the chairman of the Senate Labor Committee fails to notice the green Dodge that follows him all the way along Arlington Boulevard. Nor does he pay attention to the battered white Ford in front of him. At the Seven Corners traffic light, the car in front backs up a few feet until its rear bumper touches his own. The car behind him, in the meantime, closes in tightly. Within seconds, it is done. The white car pulls away at high speed. On the rear seat: two masked men. The senator sits between them.

Simultaneously, a telephone is ringing in the office of the Senate Labor Committee. A voice says: "Listen carefully. We do not want to hurt anybody. But unless the Senate acts to insure supplemental unemployment benefits for auto workers within the next twelve hours, we shall be forced to execute Senator Wilson. We shall be watching. As soon as the Senate approves the SUB bill, and sends it to the White House, we shall release Senator Wilson unharmed. If, after the execution of Senator Wilson, the Senate still delays approval of this bill, we shall execute another senator, and another, and another, until auto workers receive every cent that is coming to them." The wire services and television networks go beserk with the story. Within minutes the United Auto Workers at Solidarity House in Detroit issues a denunciation of the "mindless, dangerous radicals engaged in this desperate game. We have fought against such people throughout the history of our union. We are dedicated to the democratic process. The UAW hereby offers a reward of $25,000 for information leading to the arrest and imprisonment of the terrorists who today have besmirched America."

On November 1, with the crisis in the Middle East escalating, Iran in a state of total mobilization, troops patrolling the east side of Cleveland, the farm protest spreading throughout Nebraska, Kansas, Missouri, and Michigan, component shortages forcing slowdowns (and then extra-shift work) in the defense industries, coal miners in Kentucky shutting the mines down in protest against a network television comedy they regard as "dirty," the American Legion calling for "instant retaliation in Saudi Arabia," Billy Graham telling an audience of 100,000 in Nashville that "God is catching up with us," the president, in a special broadcast from the West Wing of the White House, his blue seal centered above his head, his Cabinet on either side of him, announces:

"Tonight, in view of the extreme national emergency, the dangers facing our country simultaneously from within and without, I have taken several grave but necessary actions. I have asked the Department of Defense to place all military personnel on a mobilization footing. I have given the necessary commands to federalize all National Guard units to help preserve domestic order. And I have taken the unusual step of asking the Congress of the United States and the Supreme Court jointly to approve a ninety-day delay in the forthcoming national elections. . . ."

Eco-spasm. A few additional turns of the screw, and this one might produce precisely what George Friedensohn, an international monetary consultant, expects: "The worst financial disaster of all time . . . the total destruction of money." It could produce the runs on the banks foreseen in the super-depression scenario or the widespread introduction of barter foreseen in the super-inflation scenario (perhaps accelerated, as Billy Rojas suggests, by the use of computers). It could very well lead to the breakup of many existing nations, not excepting the United States.

What we see here is a world out of control, perched on the edge of randomness. The economies of the industrial nations could easily collapse no matter which scenario plays itself out. The world is now so tightly interwired, the number of economic switches and connections so vast, that vulnerabilities have been raised to unprecedented levels. The more we have sought to build an "interdependent" highly "developed" world, the more we have raised the ante for both good and ill. In this delicately balanced situation, the third scenario, it seems to me, is more likely than the first two.

Yet even this scenario scarcely begins to capture all the probabilities. Eco-spasm could lead to severe fractures of the world trade system, as nation after nation desperately throws up tariff walls to protect its ailing industries from the wild oscillations of the world economy. It could lead to massive political shifts as well in dozens of countries simultaneously—from the rapid rise of right-wing populist groups in quasi-socialist Scandinavia to resurgent Marxism in the Mediterranean countries, to nationalist uprisings in the Soviet Union and war among the Arabs themselves. One can easily picture brutal police roundups of alien workers throughout Europe and the United States—a forced repatriation of the millions of "guest workers" who have done the dirty work in the rich countries for a decade or more—and a consequent weakening of domestic civil liberties in each of the affected countries. One can without strain imagine a British Labour government nationalizing American auto plants in Britain to prevent their closing down, while Scottish nationalist bombs wreck offshore oil rigs in the North Sea and paramilitary units arise to break strikes in Australia and New Zealand.

Beyond this, of course, lies the unthinkable: a major war. Will Kissinger and Ford charge up the beaches of Saudi Arabia, like two World War II GIs, machine guns zapping the Arabs—as a cartoon on the cover of *New York* magazine recently suggested? The caricature yields insight into our psyche. Naive and ghoulish rumors fill the air. That the U.S. Marines will polish off the recalcitrant oil producers. That Japan and Australia, both hard hit, will supply Israel with the support needed to take over the oil fields. A thirty-year guerrilla war in the deserts, with Arab terrorists carrying suitcase nuclear weapons into Chicago or Osaka or Marseilles. . . . The imagination runs riot with possibilities.

7

COPING WITH CRISIS

Of course, scenarios, no matter how plausible, remain fiction. The imagination may play with possibilities—and in considering our options it should; failure to do so is responsible for many of our difficulties. But while scenarios can help us organize our ideas, they are not "predictions" in the literal sense.

There is, for one thing, no reason to assume that angry young auto workers will kidnap a U.S. senator; they might as easily be farmers or Chicanos—or, for that matter, frustrated Algerians in Paris or Eskimos in Ottawa. There is no historic inevitability about a Saudi Arabian coup, which no doubt permits King Faisal to sleep at night; it could just as easily occur in half a dozen other Middle East countries, just as the world's first runaway fast-breeder reactor could trigger massive tragedy in the U.S. instead of the Soviet Union.

Moreover, it is fashionable today to be pessimistic. Intellectuals forecast Malthusian disaster, movies portray earthquakes and skyscraper infernos, science fiction depicts anti-utopias, and the nostalgia industry assails us with the dubious subliminal message that things were better yesterday. Certainly, the eco-spasm scenario does not paint a pretty picture. But it serves, I believe, a useful purpose because it systematically dramatizes the complexities of the crisis we face, the fact that it is not merely a traditional boom or bust, a replay of 1923 or 1929. The eco-spasm concept expands our conventional views of the problems to include all those new ecological, technological, social, and military factors that make the 1923 or 1929 comparisons so misleading.

Once having served this purpose, however, it ought not lead us to assume that the future is frozen—that only a nightmare world lies ahead. Indeed, one could write scenarios that would take account of far more positive alternatives. Such scenarios might include, for example, the discovery of a totally new source of clean energy, or an unexpected breakthrough in solar or fusion power research; the sudden rise of a religious movement in the West that restricts the eating of beef (and thereby saves billions of tons of grain and provides a more nourishing diet for the world as a whole); the invention of new transnational arrangements that defuse the nuclear arms race; or the emergence of new-style political leadership in the West that recognizes the weaknesses and inefficiencies of high centralization and moves toward peaceful regionalization and decentralization.

One might with equal justification project into these future histories the spread of humane alternatives to the assembly line; the sharing of economic power with workers and consumers; the diffusion of values that provide women with socially acceptable alternatives to childbearing roles (and thereby begin to reduce population and resource use in what we still anachronistically think of as "industrial" nations).

One might speculate about the development of a cancer cure, for example, or alternative sources of cheap protein. Some chemical in baby food might turn out to enhance, rather than retard, mental development. It is not impossible that breakthroughs in fish farming and algae cultivation will begin to improve the world hunger picture; that thermal pollution will be re-routed on a large scale into the heating of homes; that space probes will bring back clues to wholly unexpected resources; that economist E. F. Schumacher's slogan "Small Is

Beautiful" will catch on and that imaginative uses of intermediate technology will create stable, life-supporting economies in many parts of the so-called third world; that gerontologists will discover ways to prolong health during the last decades of life; that new saints and prophets will emerge to articulate the transformed values of the coming super-industrial civilization.

The truth is that we are not helpless. The emerging future is not predestined; it is the outcome of decisions taken by us in the present. Even now we can take intelligent steps to regain control over our runaway fate— and the eco-spasm scenario, precisely because it is so pessimistic, helps us to pinpoint the changes that must be made and the transition strategies that might ease our passage into the future.

Two principles or "lessons" emerge sharply from the investigations that have led to this report. They are simple and starkly self-evident. Yet my travels and interviews convince me that both are being violated every day by politicians, government officials, economists and others who, faced with the prospect, even the reality, of eco-spasm, are frantically trying to construct a new Maginot Line.

The first principle can be stated succinctly: *Economics alone cannot solve the crisis.*

Many of our immediate problems arise from trying to achieve economic goals, such as a fixed growth-rate or full employment, without worrying about other parts of the eco-system. Had we considered in advance the possibility of an energy squeeze, had we tried to foresee the impact of certain technologies on the environment, had we considered how welfare economics undermines family life and community organization, we might not now be as trapped as we are.

We know, after a decade of painful disclosures, that we live in an extremely fragile, infinitely interconnected eco-system that can be destroyed if we are not careful. The "new economics" that are necessary for curing the eco-spasm condition cannot be divorced from this looming, inescapable truth.

This means that any attempt to weaken environmental controls as a trade-off for immediate jobs or profits may deepen rather than solve the crisis. It is an attempt to mortgage—perhaps even bankrupt—the future for the sake of the moment. The reckless crash program aimed at proliferating fast-breeder nuclear reactors, for example, as a fix for the energy shortage, raises the likelihood of a disaster on a scale so hideous that it could set back further technological development and economic stability by a generation.

To permit renewed use of high-sulfur coal, to shrug aside the danger of oil slicks (while racing to develop offshore reserves), to allow aerosol deodorants and hair sprays to tear holes in the earth's ozone layer, to continue blindly to pump chemical additives, colors, and dyes into our foods so they will sell better, in short, to believe that we must sacrifice health and safety to keep our jobs (instead of holding our jobs to ensure our health and safety) is absurdly counterproductive.

It is not the physical ecology alone that must be taken into account before we seize on any economic program for dealing with the crisis. There is, in addition, a "social ecology" that must be considered. For example, attempts to maintain high efficiency in industry by repeatedly relocating workers may bring with it intractable social dislocations, family stress, the death of communities, and other negative effects.

The idea of a quick "economic fix" is just as dangerous as the comparable idea, popular among certain narrow scientists, that there is for each of our difficulties a neat, quick "technological fix."

This suggests that any economic program put forward

by a government, political party, corporation, trade union, or citizens' group ought to be immediately discounted if it fails to carry with it, in effect, an "impact statement" telling what its enactment is likely to do to the air, water, and other natural resources upon which survival depends, as well as how it might be expected to affect our family, social, and community structures. No doubt we must on occasion make trade-offs between immediate economic gain and long-term social and ecological health. But, if we do, we ought to know in advance what these trade-offs are likely to entail. Only in this way can we avoid the dangers of "econo-think"— our traditional failure to see how economics interconnect with other systems—social, cultural, and ecological. Such "impact statements" attached to all economic legislation, and to all proposed major economic policies could save us from dangerous "boomerang" effects.

Because the eco-spasm is more than just an economic problem, any attempt to deal with it as such, applying exclusively economic remedies that ignore side effects, will merely make it worse. What we will need, therefore, will be a whole battery of compatible policies dealing not only with money supply, wages, prices, and balance of payments, but with everything from resource use and environment to education and cultural life, from transport and communications to the changing relationships between men and women.

The second principle is equally brief: *The past cannot (and should not) be recaptured.* If the eco-spasm analysis is even approximately correct, and the present emergency is part of a process by which industrial societies break through to a new, more advanced stage of development, then our policies must not simply attempt to reinstate the old industrial order.

Policies aimed at putting things back where they were

—"restoring" jobs, putting more cars on the road, continuing surburban development, encouraging social standardization, cementing the nuclear family back together again in its traditional form—are reactionary whether they are espoused by the equally obsolete left, right, or center.

Of course we shall need jobs, transportation, housing, social integration, and families. But not the same jobs, the same kind of transport, the same housing, the same social policies or family structures that we have had until now.

As the crisis deepens, we will hear ever more panicky calls for a return to yesterday. On one side, the French employers' association, the Patronat, urges a new lunge at unrestrained economic growth (growth, as they call it, *à la Japonaise*).* This mentality, which has its counterpart in every country, seeks to solve the immediate crisis by applying again and with greater force the very strategies that led us into it in the first place.

Such groups have learned nothing from the past decade about the delicate balance of the world ecology, about the rising power of the developing nations, and about changed values within the dying industrial society. Their image of a desirable world is the world of the past. They are "reversionists."

For a French reversionist, the "good life" may be represented by the world of 1967—when de Gaulle was still in his glory, when students had not yet struck up barricades in the streets, when the only problem seemed to be how to catch up with the Americans in the technological growth game. For the U.S. reversionist, the year may be 1960, when a young president could speak about a New Frontier (meaning an extension of the old

---

* The Patronat's lack of irony here is decidedly non-Gallic. If there is one thing *les Japonais* know now, it is that their unbridled economic growth of the 1960s has contributed to their present severe distress.

New Deal), when affluence seemed to beckon endlessly —a promising world soon to be shattered by assassinations, marches, riots, and a gangrenous war brought home. For the Japanese the year may be 1970, when the Sato government and outside consultants could forecast straight-line economic growth until, by the year 2000, Japan would be a "super-state."

Every country and every social group has its own particular "fantasies of return." And not all of them are based on technological growth. Certain fringe ecologists are quite as reversionist in their thinking, and reach even farther back for their image of the good life. Some believe society should renounce almost all technology and return not to successful industrialism, but, indeed, to a pastoral pre-industrial status. For others, a restoration of 1920 or 1940 would do nicely—a world in which, supposedly, the air was still passably clean and pedestrians safe on the street. Among these reversionists there is a strong streak of Protestant asceticism, a feeling that affluence itself is corrupt. Some wish not simply to restore a cleaner environment but the puritanical, immobile, stagnating village society of the past. Properly disgusted with the waste, excess, and conspicuous consumerism they see around them, they look upon poverty as somehow ennobling—a view not enthusiastically shared, however, among the poor.

Both these options—technomania and unrestrained economic growth on the one hand, technophobia and romantic ruralism on the other—seek to bring back yesterday. The way up from eco-spasm is not, however, by tunneling down to the past. It is through recognition that any great crisis is also an opportunity. We should use this opportunity to propel us into a desirable, super-industrial future.

8

TRANSITION STRATEGIES

Where, then, do we go from here? Or, more to the point, how? In a relatively brief report like this one, it it obviously impossible to present a fully developed, rounded set of such "transition strategies." But a beginning can be made. What follows are several such strategies. They deliberately range in scope from the long-term to the immediate, and from the global to the domestic. They are presented less with the expectation that they will be immediately acted upon than that they will illustrate an approach strategy—a coherent way of thinking about our problems. Not all of them are original. None is a cure-all. But all flow logically from the eco-spasm analysis. All are compatible with one another. And all could help us manage a more peaceful transition into the future.

STRATEGY ONE: Re-stabilize the global economy by controlling those crucial economic forces now out of control.

The nation-state can no longer cope with the basic problems posed by the shift toward super-industrialism. In economic terms, the nation-state is a product of the industrial revolution and, as such, has served its purpose. In the technically advanced countries (if not in the developing areas) it is now fundamentally obsolete. It will not disappear, but it will shrink in power. Indeed, it already has. If the eco-spasm analysis does anything, it reveals the pitiful, bumbling incapacity of national governments and their politicians to deal with new economic forces that transcend national boundaries.

Among these forces, the absolutely crucial one is the multinational corporation. Certainly, if Eurodollars are really to function as a transnational currency their status as such must be explicitly recognized and they must be subjected to transnational control. Equally, if globe-straddling banks are to be allowed to operate, they, too, must be brought under some form of transnational regulation. But it is the multinational corporation that is "the link that pulls the chain." Without it, in all likelihood, there would be no large transnational banks or Eurodollar problem.

The multinationals are, therefore, the key to restabilizing the global economy. They represent fantastic potentials for raising living standards or for destroying them, for enhancing global awareness or for imposing their own totalitarian order. (I am reminded of a conversation I had in Tokyo with the chairman of one of Japan's giant financial houses. "We could solve so many problems," he sighed, "if we had only one big multinational corporation!")

It has been argued that the multinational corporation is itself a product of the dying industrial commitment to linear growth and that we may soon move toward new kinds of production based on greater decentralization, smaller production units, and low-energy technologies. This argument ought not be brushed hastily aside as either utopian or romantic. But whether or not that turns out to be the case over the long term, it is clear that within the *immediate* time frame—the next half decade or more—the enormous power of the multinational corporation cannot be allowed to run unchecked. Moreover, it will not.

Individual nation-states, merely to hang on to their own power a bit longer, will be forced to create new transnational control mechanisms. Politicians of individual nations will continually deny to the public that they are "surrendering sovereignty." But they will be compelled to do just that by the force of the new economics.

Indeed, the great, earth-spanning corporations will soon find it in their own interests to support the creation of some form of transnational regulatory order. Like all large organizations, they despise and fear unpredictability. They will therefore come to support some form of stabilizing machinery. A fundamental political struggle of the years ahead will be over the exact *nature* of this machinery, and the degree to which it is made accountable to public, as distinct from purely private, interests.

For, taken as a whole, the rise of the global business enterprise means a significant loss of democracy within the major industrial powers. As more and more economic decisions elude the control of the nation, they also elude democratic accountability. The very notion of democracy presupposes that the people of a country can control their own economic life. When this ceases to be true, for whatever reason, they become colonies.

In this sense, the richest countries of the world are sliding into the status of colonies. It is not only a question of oil sheikhs buying up real estate in various industrial countries or reversing the flow of foreign investment. To the degree that this happens, the risk of reverse colonialism may exist—but it remains traditional colonialism: one country subordinating the economic life of another to its own purposes. What is increasingly possible today is a new, far more slippery kind of colonalism, a super-colonialism in which national economies are subordinate not to other nations but to the workings of a transnational economic system or network over which they have no control.

What is needed now is action to de-colonize the richest and ostensibly most powerful nations as well as the poorest.

Specifically, it is time for national and local corporations to wake up to their own interests. Even the largest companies suffer when the economy is repeatedly rocked by blows from outside. Business leaders in the industrial countries now ought to join up with trade unions, consumer/environmentalist organizations, and other popular groups to press for something that is in the interests of all: regulation of the multinationals.

This may well mean enforceable supra-national or regional rules about environmental protection; wage and safety standards; transnational investment and banking; and even taxation. It may require the creation of transnational control commissions funded by taxes based on the savings that the multinationals make by being able to escape or minimize national tax obligations. (Properly taxing the multinationals would also help other companies compete more fairly with them.) It may mean requiring the global corporations to contribute to transnational funds for social development in the countries, especially the developing countries, in which they operate.

Whatever form these regulations ultimately take, the fight to control these corporations and the banks and other financial institutions that serve them, cannot be waged in any one country. The time has come to form a truly transnational political movement—bringing together workers, consumers, small business, corporate executives, ecologists, political leaders, and others *from many countries* for a new kind of global political action, a World Association for Control of Transnational Systems. Any such movement could expect immediate and substantial support from the poor nations, who also need, even more urgently, to bring the new giants into some sensible regulatory framework.

Multinational corporate executives, bankers, and money people are not sinister characters out of some *Pravda* cartoon. They are not all spies and counter-revolutionary saboteurs as the IT&T role in Chile suggests. They are simply investors, managers, and planners taking advantage of the world's biggest legal loophole—and upsetting the world economy in the process. Many multinationals have made distinct contributions to improved living standards in the countries in which they operate; some have introduced humane super-industrial work patterns; others have even, to a slight degree, begun to democratize the work place. But if we are to put together a new, more stable economic order, that is not continually jolted by gigantic, galvanic forces over which even the global corporations themselves have little systematic control, the multinationals must be regulated. The developing nations know this. It is time that we in the industrial nations, too, recognize how heavily our fate depends on it and take appropriate action.

STRATEGY TWO: Build super-industrial stabilizers to replace or supplement those that are now obsolete.

It is not merely oscillations in the money system generated by the rise of the multinationals that need to be contained. The day is now over when cheap energy and raw materials flowed in a smooth, reliable stream from the poor countries to the rich. Whatever the outcome of present economic struggles over oil, for the next half decade, at least, we must expect increasing disruptions, surges, and price oscillations. In the words of a recent report of the (U.S.) National Academy of Sciences, we face "a series of shocks of varying severity as shortages occur in one material after another. . . ." The old resource/energy bargain basement is closed. Nor, with Russia, China, India, France, and who knows how many other powers armed with nuclear weapons, is it likely to be reopened by gunboat diplomacy. Even small, non-nuclear countries are increasingly capable of self-defense, as the invasion of Cuba and the Vietnam War suggest.

This means that, as the industrial countries advance into super-industrialism they will have to base their continued affluence on something other than plentiful raw materials: an increased ability to do, as Buckminster Fuller puts it, "more with less."

While it does not mean the end of technological advance, it does mean radical conservation policies. It means a high order of imagination. And it means that tax and other incentives ought to be placed on the rapid development of low-energy and resource-conserving products. Instead of awarding indiscriminate tax credits for corporate investment, why not target these specifically for investments in new, ecologically sound, socially valuable technologies?

But the eco-spasm analysis also suggests an urgent need for new kinds of stabilizers. Since we must expect increasingly wild swings in world food and resource supplies, it is time to begin building global, as well as regional and local, food and resource stabilizers in the form of reserve stockpiles.

Stockpiles can not only help tide us over dangerous periods of shortage, but can be used intelligently to even out price oscillations when they get out of hand. (When the price of some resource is too low, the stockpiling agency, public or private, buys, supporting the price level; when prices soar because of undersupply, the agency sells, lowering the price level.)

Such a system provides a margin of insurance and stability. It protects producers and sellers against disastrous losses and, by the same token, eliminates the likelihood of extortionate profits.

At the World Food Conference in Rome in 1974 an agreement in principle was reached on the need for an internationally coordinated system of national food reserves. Such a system, calling for a buffer stock of some 60 million tons of rice, wheat, corn, sorghum, millet, and other grains, could play a vast, positive role in evening out economic swings while simultaneously helping to solve the worsening world food crisis.

Creation of this world network—and its regional counterparts—ought to receive high priority in any industrial country interested in stabilizing its own economy.* The issue of stockpiles and reserves, however, extends far beyond food alone. In the 1950s, after the Korean War, the United States maintained a stockpile of strategic materials like tungsten, bauxite, natural rubber, tin, chrome ore, and ferro-manganese. The principle behind this was not economic but military. Its purpose was to assure the U.S. a sufficient supply of strategic materials to wage war for five years. In the late 1950s this was cut back to a three-year reserve on the ground that any major war was likely to be nuclear and therefore short.

---

* To build up domestic reserves, however, without aggravating inflation, we must at the same time stimulate farm production in the developing nations. This suggests that the industrial countries should increase, not decrease, their agricultural development aid to the poorer countries, and that we ought to lift any remaining restrictions on the sale of fertilizer to developing nations.

Several industrial nations, including the U.S., have restricted exports of fertilizer in the vain effort to check rising food prices in their home markets. This was not only shortsighted but selfish. The U.S. uses so much fertilizer at present that it faces a diminishing return per ton applied. The application of the same tonnage to the fields of less technologically advanced countries might, across the board, yield a better percentage return. Also, a significant fraction of fertilizer in the industrial societies goes for non-agricultural purposes. While millions face starvation, it helps keep cemeteries, golf courses, and front lawns green.

In the early 1970s, the Nixon administration further reduced the stockpile to a one-year supply. It acted presumably in response to economic pressures: with the U.S. balance of payments problem growing worse, cutting into the stockpile rather than buying abroad reduced the outflow of dollars. Moreover, higher interest rates meant that it was costing more to maintain the reserves.

Since the wave of shortages in 1973 the idea of a stockpile with an economic, rather than merely military, purpose has drawn increasing attention in the Congress and the White House. The idea is similarly being explored in other countries, especially in light of the Arab oil embargo during the Yom Kippur War.

The stockpile concept raises difficult ideological as well as purely practical questions, especially in capitalist economies. But, whether we are speaking of food or materials, there are ways around these difficulties. In the U.S., perhaps, individual corporations could be encouraged to maintain larger inventories by permitting them to write off, for tax purposes, part of the cost of resource purchases at the time of purchase rather than at the time the materials are used in manufacture. This tax system is now employed in Sweden. By holding somewhat larger inventories, companies can buy more when prices are down and hold out longer when prices are up, thus damping somewhat the effects of rapid and steep oscillations.

Such accumulations in the private sector could be supplemented by direct government reserves. We could, moreover, create government-owned or joint public-private stand-by facilities for emergency production of essential materials. One can imagine such facilities also set up transnationally—owned by consortiums of governments and providing essential backup in case of economic or other emergency.

Such a system would require, from the outset, participation by poor nations as well as rich, producers as well as consumers. It offers a way of alleviating some of the worst instabilities afflicting the low technology world. It also offers a long-range counter to the power of exploitative cartels. At the same time, one can even imagine applying the stockpiling principle to protecting major urban areas against certain kinds of breakdown or shortage that might endanger their existence.

What does a city require to maintain what the Singapore economist Augustine Tan calls an "irreducible minimum" economy? For Singapore, hard-pressed by economic forces from outside and lacking resources of her own, except for a magnificent harbor, the issue is not academic during a global eco-spasm. Nor is it a trivial issue for other urban centers. Were urban areas and other economic regions to begin systematically assessing their rock-bottom requirements, it might be possible for us to start building "urban insurance" programs that could prove invaluable in case of large-scale systems failure, food shortages, and other life-endangering crises.

Ancient cities lived, as Kenneth Boulding has pointed out, a few weeks away from starvation. Contemporary cities are also highly vulnerable, albeit in far more subtle ways: they are so totally dependent upon external sources of food and power, on road transport, on lighting, elevators, air conditioning, heating systems, on ready supplies of oxygen for their hospitals, water for their homes and industries, on telephones and postal delivery, that they too live closer to the edge than most of us like to think about. The recent outbreak of cholera in Naples, for instance, reflects, as cholera epidemics historically have, the breakdown of public health services in times of social and economic turmoil.

As we enter a long period of social instability, we

badly need to re-examine the essentials of urban survival and begin designing urban insurance systems.

Today we see millions of frightened middle-class individuals pursuing "fallout shelter" strategies to ensure their own survival in case of disaster or breakdown. They are acquiring firearms, laying away supplies of dehydrated food, buying back-country acreage. Whether their fears are justified or not, their action reveals a profound mistrust of the ability of existing authorities to guarantee even the minima of survival.

Instead of encouraging these highly individualistic, often anti-social responses—private hoarding, for example, of products ranging from sugar to canned goods and toilet paper—we need to create a new public confidence. This cannot be done by simply labelling pessimism unpatriotic. It can be done only through social, rather than individual, transition strategies—by providing backup insurance and fail-safe devices for our threatened social and economic systems.

STRATEGY THREE: "Super-industrialize" employment policies.

Both capitalist and socialist industrial nations are supposedly committed to the idea that anyone who needs or wants a job ought to be able to find one. Today, as unemployment spreads, governments are planning to spend billions, if necessary, to prop up employment. Yet in employment policy, as in monetary and financial policy, the Maginot rule prevails: we are still fighting the last depression.

All industrial nations share certain common assumptions. Thus they base their policies on the belief that most work is done to create goods. When we think of unemployment, we automatically think of mill workers, automobile assembly-line workers, coal miners and padlocked factories. Yet it is no longer necessarily true that most people in advanced industrial nations are occupied in the manufacture of goods. Every one of these countries has witnessed pronounced shifts toward employment in the service sector, including what is coming to be known as "human services"—health, education and welfare in their myriad forms. As automation has advanced, we have, relatively speaking, de-populated our factories and shifted jobs into the white-collar and service fields. Indeed, in the U.S. it is already twenty years since service and white-collar workers began to outnumber blue-collar workers.

This shift away from the factory is part one of the transition to a super-industrial economy, and, within certain limits, ought to be strongly encouraged. Instead of devising employment policies aimed at putting people back into precisely the same jobs they have left behind, it would be far more intelligent to design selective re-employment policies that continue our conversion to a service-oriented society.

There are at least two important reasons for doing so. First, a service society can help us solve many accumulated social, community, and environmental problems bequeathed to us by the unrestrained economic growth policies of the past two decades. Second, a service-oriented society is less dependent on high imputs of energy and resources than is a traditional industrial society.

In the words of Frank Riessman and Alan Gartner, whose book *The Service Society and the Consumer Vanguard* is by far the best on this subject; "continuous industrial growth is leading to unemployment and the under-utilization of people; by contrast growth in the human services will lead to the fullest such utilization. A balanced ecological society does not call for lack of growth but rather shift to the human services. . . ."

Despite recent trends, a wide range of decent services

at acceptable price levels remain unavailable in the U.S., and even in the more welfare-oriented industrial nations. Treatment of the mentally ill and the elderly remains scandalous. Innovative education is starved. Millions of alcoholics go untreated. Prisons are a crime. There are millions of potential new jobs available in community health programs, mental health clinics, child care and geriatric centers, and in nutrition services, not to mention education of all kinds.

Outside the human services, the same is true. We lack the rudiments for sensible existence in a technological society. Anyone who has tried to get a furnace repaired, or an auto tuned up properly, or a plumbing leak plugged is aware that such services are, for all practical purposes, either unavailable or outrageously expensive.

This means that instead of imagining full employment in terms of still bigger Detroits to turn out even more unrepairable products, incentives ought to be given to developing a whole new range of services through both private and public enterprise. If someone wants to set up a small business or a franchised company to provide such elementary repair services, let us, for heaven's sake, provide special loans, credits, and other aids to get him or her started. Services are labor-intensive—and that, presumably, is what full employment programs are about.

Why, for that matter, might not new schools arise that both train people for such service occupations and at the same time finance their training by actually performing services? Connected up properly with the education system, the service industry could provide dignified occupations for millions of men and women who otherwise face bleak job prospects.

New institutions of various kinds can be invented to provide urgently needed services. These can be private (part of a regulated profit sector) or government or non-

profit—or imaginative fusions of these.* The important
issues are not ideological, public versus private; the important issues are how to get the job done and how to
provide work in the process.

New services can also be linked to environmental
maintenance—to reforestation (here a lesson can be
learned from the Civilian Conservation Corps established in the U.S. during the last depression), to reclaiming land in abandoned or "orphan" strip mines, to
cleaning up rivers, controlling rats, decreasing noise,
reclaiming waste, and scores upon scores of other such
socially necessary activities.

With respect to immediate options for those who, still
caught in the old industrial system, are jobless, whose
unemployment benefits are running dry, whose pensions
are inadequate, and whose psychological personhood is
destroyed when they are not actively productive, it is
imperative that we quickly create public employment
programs. These, however, ought not be modeled on the
old depression-style public works which sought to create
uniform jobs for millions.

Such public work programs, appropriate for their era,
are now out of date. Most were based on typical industrial era assumptions. They were centralized. They demanded standardized work. They destroyed initiative.
They gave the individual no dignity and no choice. They
evoked no enthusiasm, imagination, or enterprise from
the individual.

There is a totally different way to attack the problem,
linking it directly to our clear need for certain social,
cultural, environmental, and just plain household serv-

---

* One large insurance company has been considering developing,
as part of its life-insurance package, a program of special services
for widows and widowers. Human service needs in such a setup could
be contracted out by the company for performance by local non-profit
agencies—a reverse of the more common pattern in which non-profits
buy services from corporations.

ices. Instead of attempting to employ armies of jobless workers at the national level, as many of the depression-era programs did, or to add them to the payrolls of existing bureaucracies at city, state or regional levels, as is now proposed, we could, by contrast, set up a decentralized network of "Service Centers."

Apart from a skeleton staff such centers would hire nobody. They would, instead, elicit ideas from the unemployed themselves about how the energies and talents of the jobless might best be put to work in filling the service gap. The Centers would then fund those proposed projects that seemed likely to provide the most jobs, and the most service, for the least money.

Some of the unemployed might choose to run day-care centers or to provide transportation for the handicapped and the elderly. Others might organize a small, non-profit company to do household repairs. Unemployed engineers, scientists and technicians might create new pollution-control technology or experimental solar heating systems. Teachers might set up alternative schools to teach skills not typically available, or to work with specialized sub-groups of the child population: the especially gifted, the retarded, the handicapped. Still others might provide para-professional health services, practical nursing care, pre- and post-natal assistance. Some of these new activities might require only minimum subvention to get them going, some might even turn out to be economically self-sustaining. The Service Centers program could, therefore, divert enormous amounts of creative human energy to critical service fields; it could provide jobs almost immediately; it could do so at lower costs than the traditional programs; and it could do so without setting up new, uniform, initiative-crushing bureaucracies.

There is, indeed, an existing successful model for such an innovative policy. In Canada the so-called Local

Initiatives Program (LIP), while not specifically limited to providing services, operates very much in this way. It invites the unemployed to come up with proposals for projects that will provide jobs and serve some useful need. It then funds the best of these projects. In this way, projects vary from place to place; they meet distinct local needs; they draw on the talents and energies of the unemployed themselves. The problem, in short, is attacked from the bottom up, rather than the top down.

In the Canadian program, as in any large undertaking, there have been disappointments as well as successes. Not all the projects work out. That must be expected in any such effort. But compared with the alternatives, it is a major improvement. For it derives from sound super-industrial principles. A "Service Center" program based on the LIP model but specifically designed to shift employment into the services, would be a vast improvement over the old, depression-style job-making programs now under discussion.

For if we are going to expand public service employment—as we no doubt must and shall—at least part of that expansion should be done in a way that moves us toward super-industrial variety rather than industrial standardization, toward the multiculture rather than back to the monoculture.

Apart from the long-term shift toward service employment, other major social changes must be taken into account. One of those has to do with the family system. During the industrial age, the nuclear family (i.e., father, mother, children, with no encumbering grandparents, uncles, aunts, or other relatives) was the standard, socially-approved family form. Divorce was relatively rare. Families were essentially patriarchal and long-lasting. It is this model on which virtually all our economic and social planning is still based.

To make a smoother transition to the next stage of development, however, we must recognize that the nuclear family in its classical form is rapidly breaking down today, not because of "loose morals" or "permissiveness," but because it no longer adequately serves the needs of much of the population. This does not mean that the nuclear family will disappear or that we ought not value it, but that new, alternative arrangements are springing up rapidly and must be reckoned with in both economic and social policy.

More and more young people, for example, are expressing a conscious desire to remain childless, and in the U.S. there is already a "National Organization of Non-Parents" that promotes this attitude on ecological, demographic, and other social grounds. Because of the high frequency of divorce, remarriage has become extremely common, creating altogether new "aggregate families" that bring together the children and relatives of each divorced partner. Less common but also significant are the new communal and other group living arrangements.

Even within the nuclear family itself fundamental changes have begun to take place in the last decade. The rapid expansion of the women's movement, since publication of Betty Friedan's *The Feminine Mystique* in the mid-sixties, has brought with it the beginnings of a redefinition of sex roles in the home, in the factory and office, as well as in public life.

This vast reshuffling of sex roles and the shift away from the nuclear family is at least as profound a change, and holds at least as many long-term economic implications, as the great waves of union organizing that established collective bargaining as an important feature of industrialism. It is a key part of the Super-Industrial Revolution, and is much further advanced than many economists and politicians suspect. Thus in the U.S. today, despite lingering myths to the contrary, a substantial sector of the population no longer lives within the nuclear family framework. In urban areas, fully 25 percent of all children are now being raised in single-parent homes—almost always by a divorced or unmarried mother. This fact has staggering implications for the economy, for marketing, for product design, for housing and education—not to mention social life generally. So common is this new pattern that organizations like "Momma" have sprung up to supply single mothers with advice, support, and the beginnings of group political consciousness. In Britain, a counterpart organization called "Gingerbread" has appeared.

Despite such rapid developments, many employers and trade union officials still retain the conventional view that women can, or should, be sacked first because they are not primary breadwinners. Thinking back to earlier booms and recessions, many economists still regard women as a labor reserve that can be moved back and forth into the work force at will. They remember the end of World War II when "Rosie the Riveter," recruited to the wartime shipyards and steel mills, meekly went home to husband and kitchen when the men returned from the battlefront.

The problem today is that in millions of homes there is no husband and no other paycheck. Any assumption that millions of women workers will docilely surrender their jobs, therefore, in a time of shrinking employment needs to be radically revised. This suggests that our employment policies for dealing with the eco-spasm must be different from all past employment policies.

As the family structure continues its rapid change, new and far more flexible work arrangements will be required. In the immediate future, ways must be found to alter customary seniority rules that result in the last hired becoming the "first fired." These rules guarantee that not only women but also racial minorities, the young, and other less-protected groups will suffer the full brunt of unemployment.

Seniority rules represent a bitterly-won attempt to introduce equity into the factory. They are among the few protections that cushion the worker against the vicissitudes of economic life. No trade union can easily surrender this principle. Nor should it, unless there are adequate alternatives to replace it. Therefore, at least for transitional periods, governments must create special incentives for workers who voluntarily give up their seniority status. These incentives could take the form of earlier social security benefits, free educational credits, tax rebates, or provision for specialized training programs. Such measures would recognize the worker's long years on the job as a valid claim on the society; at the same time it would make it possible for work to be shared rather than protectively hoarded. "Seniority alternatives" would make it possible for the employment system to come to terms with the radically altered family structure.

Such incentives must also be accompanied by a general introduction of more flexible working arrangements than the old-style factory permitted. This is part of the task of up-dating our production systems. The shift away from the traditional factory opens the possibilities—still not taken advantage of on a wide scale—of creating more fluid, varied, and open work systems. This means that employment policy should encourage "flex-time" (which permits employees, within limits, to choose their own hours). It means alternating-day patterns, staggered hours. It means the same job shared or split between a husband and a wife. It means allowing fathers and mothers to bring their children to the workplace, and providing on-site child-care centers. Eventually, it means shifting more work directly back into the home, as computer consoles and other electronic technology make that possible.

In short, instead of meeting the present crisis with employment policies attuned to yesterday's industrialism, we ought to be shaping new ones that carry us toward tomorrow's super-industrialism.

STRATEGY FOUR: "Super-industrialize" national economic policy-making.

If, as we have seen, the nation is increasingly obsolete for dealing with large-scale or global problems, it is also increasingly incapable of dealing with small-scale or local problems.

The shrinking role of the nation-state is a result of pressures from within as well as without. Thus there are, as suggested earlier, intensifying demands in many of the larger industrial nations for greater regionalization and for a "devolution" of power from the nation's capital to its regions. A few years ago, British politicians in Westminster affected amusement at the idea that Scottish or Welsh nationalism would ever amount to anything. Today they are no longer amused. Instead, plans are being drawn for a Welsh Parliamentary assembly. Scots are demanding Scottish control over North Sea oil. Similar demands for regional power are manifested in France, in the Low Countries, and by semi-secessionist pressures in Canada, Australia, and elsewhere. Even in the United States the oil crisis has begun to create sectional discord, as witness the bumper stickers last winter in Dixie protesting the Northeast's reluctance to permit offshore oil drilling: "Let the Yankee Bastards Freeze in the Dark"!

Super-industrial societies are too complex to be managed centrally in the old industrial style. As the industrial monoculture gives way to the super-industrial multiculture, the bankruptcy of uniform national policies will be ever more starkly revealed. Eco-spasm vastly strengthens the case for decentralizing economic policy.

President Ford has been ridiculed for his about-face on economic policy within a matter of a few weeks. On one occasion he remarked that anyone who expected him "to make a 180-degree turn" from deflationary to inflationary measures would be disappointed. A month later he made precisely that 180-degree switch. Poor Ford was not alone. In Tokyo politicians are trapped in the same dilemma. With inflation racing ahead at an estimated 25 percent per year and unemployment above the 1 million mark, the government hunts for uniform national policies to deal with contradictory ailments. The same eco-spastic condition exists in Paris, London, and the capitals of all other industrial nations. Edward Short, Leader of the House of Commons, warns that unless plans for shifting power downward are accelerated, the United Kingdom might be destroyed within a decade. "Those who oppose devolution should," he said, "ask themselves how much longer London can sit on the U.K. barrel . . ."

Rushing back and forth, first with "anti-inflationary" and then with "anti-recessionary" programs is obsolete. The economy no longer works that way. If the eco-spasm scenario is even roughly right, it tells us to expect radically different problems in different parts of each country, in different industries, communities, and social classes. During the traditional industrial era, nationwide policies could work because conditions were fairly uniform throughout the society, and the entire public, by and large, suffered at the same time from either a "boom" or a "bust," not both. Today the idea that national governments can solve the economic crisis by turning a single spigot in the central bank to send credit surging indiscriminately into the economy or by suddenly raising or lowering taxes for the nation as a whole is obsolete.

Giving everyone a tax rebate may provide jobs—but where and for whom? It does not guarantee support for the especially hard-pressed industries, and it probably has the simultaneous effect of worsening the inflation in the booming new coal towns of the Rocky Mountains or resort communities like those around Disneyworld. Conversely, cutting off credit by raising the prime lending rate may cool down an "overheated" inflationary economy, but it can also send credit-dependent industries into a depressionary spiral. Furthermore, none of these across-the-board measures takes account of the special environmental, social, or cultural needs of increasingly varied regions, states, and cities. Uniform nationwide economic programs are the equivalent of putting every hospital patient on the same diet.

The eco-spasm report suggests, therefore, that the time has come for national governments in Washington, Paris, Tokyo, Moscow, and London to stop trying to manage centrally what is essentially unmanageable by the old means.

Rather than attempting to fix nation-wide policies, governments ought to encourage regional, state and local economic and social planning on a much wider scale. We ought to promote the development of industry-by-industry policies, to be drawn up by companies with the participation of trade unions, consumers, and public agencies. This represents a massive, vitally needed devolution of power and will require redistribution of tax revenues downward from national to local levels.

The United States has never been quite as heavily over-centralized as most other industrial nations, and, as a result, has an opportunity to make an easier, more peaceful transition to decentralized, regionalized economic policy. It should seize that advantage.

The diversification of society, its shift from industrial homogeneity to super-industrial heterogeneity, is one of the fundamental processes of our epoch. It writes an end to the ability of governments to control or regulate national economic life from the center. A multitude of shifting, transient needs cannot be met by the "fine tuning" of experts and politicians located hundreds of geographical miles, and a million "social miles," from the reality. It can only be handled by decentralized economic intervention, locally, regionally, and sectorally determined by democratic means, and with the national government serving only to sort out the glaring contradictions and to allocate certain resources.

STRATEGY FIVE: Accelerate the move toward anticipatory democracy.

Just as the break-up of social and economic uniformity requires increasing "custom-tailoring" of economic policy, the process of acceleration demands increased "future-consciousness" and long-range thinking. The faster events move, the more it becomes necessary to anticipate, rather than merely react to, new opportunities and crises.

Today, as a consequence of the eco-spasm, governments everywhere are racing to improve their planning processes. It is no longer a question of planning versus non-planning. It is a question of staying one jump ahead of the snowballing crises. In France, in little more than a year, a Central Planning Council was set up to bypass bureaucratic intermediaries and meet frequently in the Office of the President. Meanwhile, a regional reform has divided the country into twenty-one areas and created an elected planning council in each. As the country begins to prepare its Seventh Plan, covering the years 1975–1980, these regional councils are supposed to come into play, integrating their work with that of the Central Planning Council. On yet another front, an inter-ministerial committee has been established to deal with the task of restructuring French industry.

In Britain (at the same time) even more dramatic measures are being debated. Parliament has before it an Industry Bill which proposes one of the most sweeping reforms since the end of World War II. Spearheaded by Anthony Wedgwood Benn, Secretary of State for Industry, the new policy would create a National Enterprise Board with powerful economic planning functions. The nation's 100–150 largest corporations would be encouraged to enter into three-way "planning agreements" with both government and the relevant trade unions. Through such joint plans an attempt would be made to expand corporate investment (which runs at about half the rate of investment in Japan, France or the U.S.) and to guide it into high priority channels. The measure is also designed to give workers, through their unions, some participation in corporate policy-making.

In the United States, the race to regain control over events takes a different form. Traditionally, American business has opposed governmental intervention in the economy and government planning has carried with it the stigma of "socialism." On the other hand, the very large corporations have almost all busily created their own planning units to increase their control over both production and marketing. Dividing the corporate sector into two parts, Galbraith speaks of the "planning system" comprised of large-scale enterprises, often multinational, which has considerable power to "administer" prices, and a vestigial "market system" composed of smaller, more competitive enterprises.

Among companies in the planning system, resistance to government planning has faded as they have grown more confident and cosmopolitan. Having seen that countries like Japan, France and Sweden can engage in government planning without falling into the arms of communism, there is, in fact, an undercurrent of support among top managers for increased government efforts along this line. Their concern now is for it to be properly integrated with the plans of the private sector.

The new acceptance of long-range planning is not, however, a monopoly of the corporations. As newspapers, magazines, television talk shows, and ordinary citizens voice disillusionment with the government for failing to anticipate the eco-spasm, "futures research" and other forms of long-range analysis and speculation are gaining increased public respectability as well. Not surprisingly, this sudden opinion swing is reflected in Washington.

In the executive branch, Vice President Nelson Rockefeller has announced his intention to remake the Domestic Council of the White House into a think tank for analysis of long-term national alternatives, instead of an agency devoted solely to day-to-day action. Rockefeller's own privately financed "Commission on Critical Choices for Americans," set up before he was appointed to the vice presidency, organized batteries of professors and specialists to prepare papers on various future problems facing the nation. The commission was seen, perhaps with justice, as a vehicle for Rockefeller's presidential ambitions, leading one wag to suggest that the really critical choice the commission offers Americans is between Nelson as president in 1976 or Nelson as president in 1980. But the commission, whatever its shortcomings and virtues, clearly reflects the Vice-President's concern to be publicly regarded as "future-oriented."

Rockefeller is not alone in sensing a new mood in the country and reacting to it. A former Vice-President, now back in Senate, has been gathering support for a major piece of legislation that would also have important implications for national planning. Senator Hubert Humphrey's bill, calling for a "national growth and development" agency to be created in the White House, would coordinate the work of such existing groups as the Council of Economic Advisers, the Office of Management and the Budget, and the Environmental Quality Council.

While it scants certain issues such as the quality of work and family life or the nature of political participation that should be a part of any successful policy for channeling and controlling growth, it does call for a network of regional planning commissions across the nation to facilitate coordination of national with state and local planning, along with various citizens' advisory groups. Its overall intent is to "provide for a detailed and continuous analysis of our national priorities and a coordinated system to plan for national growth. . . ."

According to Humphrey, "Crisis management has become the hallmark of our federal government today —which, of course, merely reflects its past failures to anticipate. . . . We must begin to look and plan ahead so we can minimize, if not avoid, more of these crises in the future."

This build-up of support for increased governmental attention to the future is also occurring in the legislative branch itself as part of moves to strengthen the Congress in its dealing with the White House. Last fall, in the process of reorganizing its committees the House of Representatives passed a little-noticed, but potentially significant, rule that requires most standing committees, for the first time, to assume a "foresight" function. Prodded by John Culver, an Iowa Democrat with a long-time interest in futures research, this "foresight provision" charges these committees with undertaking "systematic, long-range, and integrated study of our principal future national problems." The new Budget Committee is also charged with examining proposed White House budgets in terms of national priorities in a five-year time frame. A few years ago such proposals would have been met with derision.

Instead, this strengthening of Congressional concern with the future recently was publicly praised by a group of citizens including long-range planners and such prominent personalities as Margaret Mead, the anthropologist, Jonas Salk, discoverer of the anti-polio vaccine, Scott Carpenter, the astronaut, Betty Friedan, the feminist leader, Arthur Okun, former chairman of the Council of Economic Advisers, William Ruckelshaus, former head of the Environmental Protection Agency, and others, including the author. The foresight provision could be an important step toward introducing longer-term considerations into legislative bodies at state and local levels as well.

At the same time, however, a new lobby has appeared in Washington called the Initiative Committee for National Economic Planning. This group is spearheaded by Harvard economist Wassily Leontief, Leonard Woodcock, chief of the United Auto Workers, and—significantly—a number of representatives of big business and investment banking. Amid a flourish of publicity, the committee has begun to push for a highly centralized economic planning agency which would prepare a master plan for the U.S. economy, pass it through the White House and Congress, and suggest industry-by-industry production targets. A bill has been introduced into the Senate embodying this proposal.

The bill contains a few ritual references to "participation" and "decentralization," but it is hard-core *centralization* that its backers seek, and its emphasis is on technical inputs rather than public involvement in the planning process. The proposal in its present form provides few if any channels for ideas or negative feedback from "below." Moreover, the convergence of "big business," "big labor" and "big government" support for the measure is unsettling to some who see in it the possibility of a kind of velvet oppression from the top—"friendly fascism."

Some of the new efforts to introduce longer time-horizons into politics are overdue and welcome developments. The accelerated pace at which problems arise, the longer time periods over which large-scale projects must be funded and monitored, the burgeoning complexity of choices facing us, all demand a much greater investment in foresight, speculation, analysis, and priority-setting than has ever been required before. What is more, the growing diversity within societies moving toward super-industrial status means that this long-range thinking cannot be limited to the national level but must penetrate both business and government at state and even community levels.

Beyond this, it is now only a matter of time before these planning efforts move to the next stage—the transnational stage. It is impossible, as this report has repeatedly emphasized, for the industrial societies to solve their problems on a national basis. It is not energy alone, or Eurodollars, or multinational corporations that present problems beyond the capacity of any nation to resolve. Inflation, worker migration patterns, pollution, and scores of other issues have taken on transnational dimensions. The inflation rate of 32 percent in Yugoslavia does not arise from peculiarities of its worker-managed production system any more than that of Britain arises from internal crises alone. Poisons dumped into the Rhine by chemical companies in Switzerland pollute the river in Germany and the Netherlands. Television programs broadcast in the United States create cultural tensions in Canada.

All these tight interdependencies suggest that as intensified efforts are made to improve planning, the planners will soon be forced to move to the supra- or transnational level. France's new Central Planning Council cannot function without taking Germany's plans into account. The U.S. cannot balance its payments without advance knowledge of the plans of the Japanese for auto or electronics production.

All this, however, raises a frightening specter. In *Future Shock* I called attention to the three basic features of planning in industrial nations—an obsession with economics to the exclusion of other concerns; a time-bias that regards five years as "long-range;" and an elitist character that removes decisions from the ordinary citizen and hands them over to remote experts and bureaucrats. The necessity for more planning and foresight is inescapable. But many of the steps now being taken in the hopes of improving our control over the future are based on the old industrial mentality. Intensified and raised to transnational power, they conjure up a picture of even more centralized technocratic societies, with decisions taken at an even greater remove from the individual—and, precisely because of this, with even *less* effectiveness than at present.

For the more centralized, remote and expert-dominated the planning process becomes, the farther it moves away from the local, the less public participation there is in it, the less, not more, efficacious it becomes. The industrial mentality thinks that efficiency comes from centralization of power, ignoring the ever-increasing need for information in the system, and especially the need for negative feedback so that poor plans can continually be corrected before errors mushroom into disasters. That vital negative feedback can only come from an educated, informed, and involved public.

If we wish to improve our capacity for shaping the

future, therefore, we must begin now to move away from industrial-style planning—which is still the only style with which most planners and politicians are familiar. We need, in short, to shift from industrial-style planning to super-industrial futurism. Futurism differs from planning, if one wishes to make that distinction, by reaching beyond economics to embrace culture, beyond transportation to include in its concerns family life and sex roles, beyond physical and environmental concerns to include mental health and many other dimensions of reality. It reaches beyond the conventional time frame of the industrial style planner toward longer, 10-, 20-, or 30-year speculative horizons, without which the short-range plans make little sense. Furthermore, it seeks radical new ways to democratize the process—not merely because that is good, just, or altruistic, but because it is necessary: without broad-scale citizen involvement, even the most conscientious and expertly drawn plans are likely to blow up in our faces.

How to bring this "super-industrialization" of planning about, how to convert it from planning, as it were, to futurism is by no means a simple task. No one can rest easy about our chances. No one has a neat, simple, effective blueprint for how to do it, because it has never before been done. Nevertheless, new ways will have to be found to open the entire process, even at the highest levels, to popular input, to feedback from below. The old fob-off of "public hearings" at which various experts and official groups testify will not be enough. The old token representation of blacks, women or workers on boards will not be enough. We will need new ways to bring trade unions into the process, to assure that women's groups, ethnic groups, environmentalists and others are permitted to make contributions at every level. What will be needed are grass-roots organizations with massive public participation whose mandate is to help (and watch) the planners. Electronic polling, referenda, television "gaming," random sampling, Delphi surveys, and the appointment of "planning juries"—citizens chosen by lot to sit and work with the planners for specified periods—may have to be tried.

All this is essentially virgin territory. But there are signs we are beginning to explore it. Thus, in August, 1970, the state of Hawaii, under the sponsorship of its Democratic governor, convened a conference called Hawaii 2000.

At this meeting, several hundred teachers, executives, government officials, truck drivers, students, housewives and others undertook to consider what the urban-rural balance should be in Hawaii—in the year 2000. They debated the appropriate blend of tourism to agriculture and industry in the economy—in the year 2000. With mounting excitement and large doses of imagination, they examined education, transport, ecology, and many other issues of immediate concern—examined them not simply in terms of instant pressures but of long-term implications. This exercise in anticipatory democracy opened for public discussion so many previously unconsidered alternatives for the future of the state that it soon led to the convening of similar meetings at the county and township levels, as well as the formation of specialized groups to consider the future of justice and the penal system, as well as the overall future of the Hawaiian economy.

Since then similar anticipatory democracy activities have been held or planned in a score of states as well as various cities and regions. In Seattle, Washington, a Republican city council and a Democratic mayor jointly convened a series of city-wide meetings to produce recommendations for long-range community policy. Any citizen who showed up for 75 percent of these meetings had a right to vote on the final recommendations. The city political leaders did not agree automatically to accept the citizens' goal recommendations, but did undertake to consider and respond to them.

In Iowa, once more at the suggestion of Senator Culver, the Hawaii formula was adopted and inverted. Under the auspices of Governor Ray, a Republican, some 1,500 to 1,800 local meetings, involving an estimated 35,000 to 50,000 citizens, were held all over the state. These meetings passed proposals up to regional and then statewide assemblies. Again the fate of the state over the next quarter century received responsible, thoughtful consideration. New policies were proposed, some of which have begun to find their way into legislative packages. Elsewhere, anticipatory democracy experiments have made imaginative use of television to present long-range options to the community and of newspapers to provide ballots through which citizens could vote on these options.

In Washington State a more advanced model of democratic futurism has been attempted. There the process has been directly integrated with the State's official planning system. The planners, recognizing that they cannot do a good job without broad public involvement and support, have taken as their slogan, "You don't have to be an expert to know what you want!"

From random samples of names submitted by various voluntary organizations in the state—women's groups, trade unions, professional societies and the like—they have created 11 citizen teams charged with defining goals for the next 15 years of the state's development. These teams have generated proposals in such fields as health, housing, ecology, transport, jobs and the like; they have studied the "cross impacts," that is, the way each of these goals, if achieved, would affect the others; they have attempted to forecast the new problems that would arise if their goals were, in fact, to be attained;

they have written scenarios describing actions that could be taken to achieve the goals. They have then grouped their proposals into 11 distinct policy packages or alternatives—11 different visions of a Washington of the future.

For example, one alternative calls for Washington to remain a primarily agricultural state; a second would require a strong shift toward industrialization; a third suggests building the economy on the basis of tourism and recreation; a fourth sees the State becoming America's chief port of entry for trade and culture from the Far East. The 11 sharply different images of attainable futures were then presented on television throughout the state, and described in detail in a tabloid newspaper nearly 1,500,000 copies of which were distributed to the public. The paper contained a ballot permitting the reader to vote, item by item, for his or her preferred future.

The planners then went a step further in seeking feedback from ordinary citizens. Recognizing that many poor, uneducated, elderly or minority group people frequently fail to participate, even when invited to do so, they conducted a number of random sample surveys by both mail and, more important, by telephone. Thus they actually had an opportunity to talk directly with precisely the kinds of people who normally are silent, unrepresented, and unconsulted.

The final results of these feedback procedures were then used to guide the state in the preparation of a series of legislative proposals, many of them explicity backed by the Governor. Much of this legislation is now before the State Legislature. Indeed, a matrix has been prepared listing the various desired goals and processes preferred by the public, and *every* bill introduced into the Legislature is now measured explicitly against these goals to see whether it generally advances them or not.

The Alternatives for Washington program is now to become a regular process conducted year after year to gain a changing, dynamic image of what the citizens of the state want for their future.

Of course, this model, too, has its weaknesses; it is no panacea. But it is an unusual experiment, a social innovation that will be much studied. Designed with the assistance of the Brookings Institution, it makes far more sophisticated use of feedback processes than the centralized economic planning approach. In the years ahead we shall need to develop many other participatory planning models as well.

In state after state now, proposals are reaching the legislatures for commissions, councils or committees on the long-term future. For a politician to express an interest in the year 2000 is no longer regarded as evidence of impracticality or otherworldliness; it is a political plus. Thus we see, in the United States, at least, an incipient change in the public's awareness that could have far-reaching, positive political effects. It is by no means clear yet how important these developments are —whether they can achieve for the ordinary citizen a real say in the political planning process, whether they can help us to prevent its over-centralization and capture by technocrats imbued with the old industrial mentality. What is clear is that advance consideration of long-range future alternatives is a necessary part of any transition to the super-industrial society.

For if eco-spasm tells us anything, it is that we cannot escape the future by turning our backs on it. Foresight is uniquely human and it is essential for survival. Without this ability to imagine alternative tomorrows and to select among them, there could be no culture, no civilization. Evolution now demands a vast enhancement of this ability, not merely among a few specialists but throughout the society. For unless political foresight is brought under popular control, it could destroy us.

Under conditions of high-speed change a democracy without the ability to anticipate condemns itself to death. But an anticipatory government without effective citizen participation and, indeed, control may be no less lethal. The future must neither be ignored nor captured by an elite. Only anticipatory democracy can provide a way out of the contradiction in which we find ourselves.

Such ideas, in a moment of profound crisis, may seem utopian and impractical. No doubt these transition strategies have many faults. They are incomplete, and events may compel us to discard them and look in totally different directions. Nevertheless, it seems sensible to recognize that we have not been put in our present plight by utopians or impractical idealists. The eco-spasm is the inexorable outcome of processes controlled and set in motion by some of our most hardheaded "realists." What seemed realistic to them seems, in this schizophrenic economy, to have been perhaps impractical, shortsighted, downright foolish.

It all depends upon the perspective. For what is happening is not just some normal, linear extension of industrial society; what is happening is the beginning of its transformation. One can look at the economic death agonies of industrial civilization as unequivocally bad. Most of us reading this are products of that civilization and have large stakes in its survival: jobs, careers, power, egos. To read that it is in its twilight casts a *Götterdämmerung* gloom about us.

Yet one might also look upon the coming years of trauma as the long-needed opportunity to set some old problems straight—to overhaul some of our creaking, undemocratic political institutions; to humanize technology; to think our way through to a fresh set of both personal and political priorities. To re-examine the blind faith we have in the processes of economic integration. To think not merely about minimum living standards but perhaps about maximum ones; to move, in short, toward some concept of enoughness so that energies, imagination, and passion can begin to flow into dimensions of growth long ignored by us. To re-evaluate the notions of individualism and collectivism, seeing them not as mutually exclusive Aristotelian opposites, but as necessary to one another. To invent new institutions, family styles, fusions of work and meaning. In short, to undertake an awesome but exhilarating task that few generations in human history have ever faced: the design of a new civilization.

The years immediately ahead will no doubt be painful. But if the notion of automatic "progress" is naive, so is the notion of inevitable "retrogression." If we can look beyond the immediate, we glimpse breakthroughs to something not merely new, but in many ways better and more just. To quote Raymond Fletcher again: "All these alarming symptoms that so frighten us—they may be birth symptoms instead of death symptoms."

BIBLIOGRAPHY

Aron, Raymond, *The Industrial Society* (New York: Simon and Schuster, 1967).

Attali, Jacques and Guillaume, Marc, *L'Anti-économique* (Paris: Presses Universitaires de France, 1974).

Barnet, Richard J., and Müller, Ronald E., *Global Reach, the Power of the Multinational Corporations* (New York: Simon and Schuster, 1974).

Bendiner, Robert, *Just Around the Corner, a Highly Selective History of the Thirties* (New York: Harper & Row, 1967).

Bird, Caroline, *The Invisible Scar, the Great Depression, and What It Did to American Life, from Then Until Now* (New York: David McKay, 1966).

———, *Everything a Woman Needs to Know to Get Paid What She's Worth* (New York: David McKay, 1973).

Boulding, Kenneth E., *Principles of Economic Policy* (Englewood Cliffs, N. J.: Prentice-Hall, 1958).

———, *The Meaning of the Twentieth Century* (New York: Harper & Row, 1964).

Brenner, M. Harvey, *Mental Illness and the Economy* (Cambridge, Mass.: Harvard University Press, 1973).

Brown, Lester R., *World Without Borders* (New York: Random House, 1972).

———, *In the Human Interest, a Strategy to Stabilize World Population* (New York: W. W. Norton, 1974).

Browne, Harry, *How You Can Profit from the Coming Devaluation* (New York: Avon, 1971).

———, *You Can Profit from a Monetary Crisis* (New York: Bantam, 1975).

Burton, Theodore E., *Financial Crises and Periods of Industrial and Commercial Depression* (Wells, A.: Fraser, 1966; orig. pub., 1902).

Clark, Wilson, *Energy for Survival* (Garden City, N.Y.: Doubleday Anchor, 1974).

Clough, Shepard B., Moodie, Thomas, and Moodie, Carol, eds., *Economic History of Europe: Twentieth Century* (New York: Harper & Row, 1968).

Daly, Herman E., *Toward a Steady-State Economy* (San Francisco: W. H. Freeman, 1973).

Freedman, Alfred M., M.D., and Kaplan, Harold I., M.D., eds., *Comprehensive Textbook of Psychiatry* (Baltimore: Williams & Wilkins, 1967).

Freedman, Alfred M., M.D., Kaplan, Harold I., M.D., and Sadock, Benjamin J., M.D., *Modern Synopsis of Psychiatry* (Baltimore: Williams & Wilkins, 1972).

Fritsch, Albert J., *The Contrasumers, a Citizen's Guide to Resource Conservation* (New York: Praeger, 1974).

Galbraith, John Kenneth, *Economics and the Public Purpose* (Boston: Houghton Mifflin, 1973).

Gartner, Alan and Riessman, Frank, *The Service Society and the Consumer Vanguard* (New York: Harper & Row, 1974).

Goldston, Robert, *The Great Depression* (Greenwich, Conn.: Fawcett, 1968).

Hutchison, Robert A., *Vesco* (New York: Praeger, 1974).

Klein, Donald F., M.D., and Davis, John M., M.D., *Diagnosis and Drug Treatment of Psychiatric Disorders* (Baltimore: Williams & Wilkins, 1969).

Leinsdorf, David, and Etra, Donald, *Citibank* (New York, Grossman, 1973).

Little, Jane Sneddon, *Euro-dollars* (New York: Harper & Row, 1974).

Mandel, Ernest, *Decline of the Dollar, a Marxist View of the Monetary Crisis* (New York: Monad, 1972).

Mayer, Martin, *The Bankers* (New York: Weybright and Talley, 1974).

McHale, John, *The Ecological Context* (New York: George Braziller, 1970).

Meadows, Donella H., Meadows, Dennis L., Randers, Jørgen and Behrens, William W., III, *The Limits to Growth* (New York: Universe, 1972).

Mesarovic, Mihajlo, and Pestel, Eduard, *Mankind at the Turning Point, the Second Report to the Club of Rome* (E. P. Dutton / Reader's Digest Press, 1974).

Moonman, Eric, *Reluctant Partnership* (London: Victor Gollancz, 1971).

Moonman, Eric, ed., *Science and Technology in Europe* (Harmondsworth, England: Penguin, 1968).

Odum, Howard T., *Environment, Power, and Society* (New York: Wiley-Interscience, 1971).

Passell, Peter, and Ross Leonard, *The Retreat from Riches, Affluence and Its Enemies* (New York: Viking, 1971).

Poor, Riva, ed., *4 Days, 40 Hours* (New York: New American Library, 1973).

Raw, Charles, Page, Bruce, and Hodgson, Godfrey, *"Do You Sincerely Want to Be Rich?"* (New York: Bantam, 1972).

Reinmann, Guenter, *The Future of the Dollar* (New York: International Reports, 1971).

Ringer, Fritz K., *The German Inflation of 1923* (New York: Oxford University Press, 1969).

Robbins, Lord, and others, *Inflation: Economy and Society* (London: Institute of Economic Affairs, 1972).

Roepke, Wilhelm, *Economics of the Free Society* (Chicago: Henry Regnery, 1963).

Samuelson, Paul A., *Economics,* 8th ed. (New York: McGraw-Hill, 1970).

Schmalz, Anton B., ed., *Energy: Today's Choices, Tomorrow's Opportunities* (Washington, D. C.: World Future Society, 1974).

Schumacher, E. F., *Small Is Beautiful a Study of Economics as If People Mattered* (London: Blond & Briggs, 1973).

Segal, Ronald, *The Decline and Fall of the American Dollar* (New York: Bantam, 1974).

Servan-Schreiber, J.-J., *The American Challenge* (New York: Avon, 1969).

Staff, Robert J., and Tannian, Francis X., *Externalities: Theoretical Dimensions of Political Economy* (New York: Dunellen, 1972).

Stephenson, Hugh, *The Coming Clash, the Impact of Multinational Corporations on National States* (New York: Saturday Review Press, 1973).

Teweles, Richard J., Harlow, Charles V., and Stone, Herbert L., *The Commodity Futures Trading Guide* (New York: McGraw-Hill, 1969).

Theobald, Robert, *The Guaranteed Income* (Garden City, N. Y.: Doubleday, Anchor, 1967).

Turner, Louis, *Multinational Companies and the Third World* (New York: Hill and Wang, 1973).

Vacca, Roberto, *The Coming Dark Age* (New York: Doubleday, 1973).

Ward, Benjamin, *What's Wrong with Economics?* (London: Macmillan, 1972).

INDEX

acceleration, 14, 22, 24, 32, 33, 35, 38, 46
accounting, 13
adaptation, 22, 33
advertising, 23, 38
aerosol, 70
affinity groups, 31
agro-corporations, 37, 57
Alaska, 40
algae cultivation, 68
Algerians, 67
alienation, 29
Allende, Salvador, 13
Allies, 39, 42
Alsace, 40
AFL-CIO, 59
American Legion, 64
amphetamine, 33
Anaconda Copper, 11
Annabel's, 53
annual reports, 6
anticipatory democracy, 95, 100–104
apocalyptic views, 1–3, 20
Arabs, 11, 17, 19, 28, 36, 42, 54, 57, 65–66, 81
Aramco Marine Terminal, 60
Arizona, 43
art forms, 32
Asia, 10
assembly line, 21
Atlanta, Georgia, 61
Austin (Texas), 61
Australia, viii, 43, 44, 65
Austria, 9n, 12

Bahamas, 10
balance of payments, 10, 14, 15, 17, 81
Bangladesh, 26
Bank Credit Analyst, 8
Bank of England, 7, 9
Bankers, The, 7
Bankhaus, Herstatt, 8
banking, 4, 5, 6–13, 15, 17, 23, 27, 33, 34, 45–46; *see also* central banks
bankruptcy, 2–3, 43–44, 56
Barrons, 24
barter, 41
Bayer, 12
Beirut (Lebanon), viii
Belgium, 10, 15, 21, 92
Bell Telephone System, 54
Benn, Anthony Wedgwood, 96
Berkeley, 49
Beverly Hills, 41, 57
Birmingham (G.B.), 53
black markets, 37
black workers, 55, 101
Boettinger, Henry, 54
Bogotá, 1

bolshevism, 42
Bosch, Hieronymous, 2
Boulding, Kenneth, 82
Brazil, 5
breakdowns, *see* systems failures
Bretons, 21
Bretton Woods (N.H.), 14
British Columbia, 21
British Labour government, 65
British Parliament, 26, 53, 96
British Petroleum, 12
Buchenwald, 3
Buffalo (N.Y.), 54, 55
Burpee Seed Company, 56
business cycle, 4
Business Week, 22

Calais, 26, 37
California, 2, 40, 45, 56, 62
Canada, 21, 25, 56, 87–88, 99
cancer cure, 68
Cantor, Eddie, 49
capitalism, 3, 15, 20, 31, 42, 75
Caribbean, 55
cartels, 17, 27, 28, 36, 82
Cayman Islands, 5
Cedar Rapids (Iowa), 54
central banks, 4, 7, 9–11, 15, 23, 93; *see also* Federal Reserve Bank, et. al.
centralization, 100
CERN (Conseil Europeen pour la Recherche Nucleaire), 62
Chamber of Commerce, 21
Chase Manhattan Bank, 59
Chicago, 10, 40, 55, 66
Chicanos, 67
childrearing, *see* family
Chile, 78
China, 62, 79
Citibank, *see* First National City Bank
cities, *see* urban areas
Civilian Conservation Corps (U.S.), 86
class interests, 20
Cleveland (Ohio), 55, 59, 60, 63
coal, 18, 19, 56
Coca-Cola, 11
Colombo, Emilio, 54
colonialism, 20, 21, 51, 76
Colorado, 56
Columbus (Ohio), 61
Coming Dark Age, The, 25
commercial paper, 38
Commission on Critical Choices for Americans, 97, 98
commodity market, 24–25
communications, 3, 5, 6, 12, 22, 32
communism, 3, 20
computers, 2, 4, 6, 9, 12–13, 33
ConAgra, 57

111

ABOUT THE AUTHOR

ALVIN TOFFLER is the author of *Future Shock,* hailed as one of the most influential books of the decade. Translated into some twenty languages, it has sold 6 million copies and been published in fifty countries. Formerly associate editor of *Fortune* and Visiting Scholar at the Russell Sage Foundation, Mr. Toffler has taught at Cornell University and contributed to scholarly journals as well as popular magazines from *Esquire* and *Playboy* to the *Reader's Digest*. He holds honorary doctorate degrees in science, letters and law.

Bantam Book Catalog

It lists over a thousand money-saving best-sellers originally priced from $3.75 to $15.00 —bestsellers that are yours now for as little as 60¢ to $2.95!

The catalog gives you a great opportunity to build your own private library at huge savings!

So don't delay any longer—send us your name and address and 25¢ (to help defray postage and handling costs).